THE SECOND COMING OF JESUS CHRIST

THE SECOND COMING OF JESUS CHRIST

*A study of the doctrine of
the Second Coming of Jesus Christ*

Kevan Kingsley Clawson

Walking the Line Publications South Jordan, Utah

Other books by Kevan Clawson
Psalms to the Lord
The Atonement of Jesus Christ
A Life of Miracles
Becoming a Great Missionary

Books by Kevan & Terri Clawson
Obtaining Your Calling and Election

Cover Photo: Elizabeth Clawson
Cover Design: Jaime Clawson
Electronic Page Makeup Jennifer Asplund
Editing: John Hopkins
Printer and Binder: Printed in the USA by Morris Publishing, 3212 E. Highway 30, Kearney, NE 68847, (800) 650-7888

Distributed by Walking the Line Publications, P.O. Box 95645, S. Jordan, UT 84095–0645
www.walkingthelinebooks.com

ISBN 0-9714540-2-7

Dedicated to my children:

Michael, Jeremiah, Isaac, Seth, and Elizabeth

*With the firm hope that we will all be taken up
to meet in the clouds of heaven
at the Second Coming of our Lord Jesus Christ*

Contents

Introduction

The greatest event that will occur in our dispensation of time will be the Second Coming of the Lord Jesus Christ. The scriptures are full of prophecies concerning this event and the signs that will precede it. In this discourse, I have tried to follow the written scriptures in a logical manner. Where contradictions or discrepancies occur, I have sought out commentary from modern day prophets. When all else failed, I have given latter-day scripture precedence over ancient scripture.

Obviously, the complexity and number of specific events or signs that will occur prior to the Second coming prevent anyone from delineating the exact sequence of events to take place. I have simply tried to place them in a sequence of time and place that both agrees with the written word and will bring understanding to the reader. *Whether the events occur in the exact manner I have laid out does not matter.* If the reader finally grasps the magnitude of the events to take place, and receives a basic understanding of the specific signs to look for (and look forward to), then I will have accomplished my purpose.

There are three keys I have discovered in coming to an understanding of the Second Coming:

1. *There will be many visits of Jesus Christ to the earth in the Last Days; these appearances* together *comprise the "Second Coming."* [1]
2. *The gospel will be preached in all the world prior to the Second Coming. There are three great divisions or time periods in accomplishing this goal: the* Times of the Gentiles, *the* Times of the Jews, *and the* Times of the Heathen Nations. *Each period has a specific and unique event or sign that starts or ends each division of time.*
3. *Most of the plagues, wars, and celestial upheavals that will occur can be classified into three greater events called in the scriptures "Woes:" the first woe (a star falls to earth), the second woe (the war of Armageddon), and the third woe (Jesus Christ). Almost all of the destructive events destined to come upon men in the last days are a direct result of these three events.*

There are hundreds, even thousands, of scriptural references that talk about the Second Coming of Jesus Christ. Rather than burden the reader with endless quotes, I have chosen to give just one or two references for each event or concept—just enough to give you a flavor of, and confidence in, the sequence of events as I have outlined them.

---

[1] Bruce R. McConkie, *Millennial Messiah*, Chapter 19:230. "This coming—and there will be many appearances which taken together comprise the second coming of the Son of Man—this coming will be in the midst of war . . . ."

THE SECOND COMING
OF JESUS CHRIST

Chapter One
Preaching the Gospel to All the World

Prior to the coming of Christ, the gospel must be preached in all the world to prepare and warn the Children of God of Christ's Second Coming.[1]

> *"And again, this Gospel of the Kingdom shall be preached in all the world, for a witness unto all nations, and then shall the end come, or the destruction of the wicked." (Joseph Smith Translation Matthew verse 31)*

This missionary work will occur in three great periods or "times": 1) the *Times of the Gentiles,* 2) the *Times of the Jews* (or Israel), and 3) the *Times of the Heathen Nations.*

Each of these periods of time has very specific events, or "signs," that will occur to let the faithful know of God's hand in these great earthly events. For those who believe in Christ and are diligently watching for his return, these "signs" will become beacons of light, confirming their faith and preparing them for the day when he will come again.

---

[1] See Note 1

1

THE TIMES OF THE GENTILES

The first major "missionary" period of time in the Last Days is called the *Times of the Gentiles*. The event or sign that begins this first missionary period, and in fact begins the era of time called "the Last Days,"[2] is the visit of the Father and Son to Joseph Smith.

> *"And when the times of the Gentiles is come in, a light shall break forth among them that sit in darkness, and it shall be the fullness of my gospel." (D&C 45:28)*

The calling of a new prophet, the translation of the Book of Mormon, and the establishment of The Church of Jesus Christ of Latter-day Saints prepared the way for the fullness of the Gospel to be restored in our day.[3] The appearance of God the Father and his Son Jesus Christ to Joseph Smith started the period of time anxiously awaited by all of the Prophets since the time of Adam—the latter-days and the restoration of all things. Once a Prophet was called and the Gospel was restored to the earth, the preaching of that Gospel began the missionary period known as the Times of the Gentiles. This period of time was to last one generation, or about 100 years.[4]

> *"And in that generation shall the times of the Gentiles be fulfilled." (D&C 45:30)*

> *"In the sense of measuring time by the lives of men, a generation, since the Abrahamic day, has been about 100 years." (Mormon Doctrine, p. 310, Generation)*

The focus of missionary work during this first period of time would be centered in the "Gentile Nations" of North America and Europe.[5] After the Gospel is given to—and rejected by—the Gentiles, it will be *through* the Gentiles that the Gospel is eventually sent to the Jews and the other Tribes of Israel.

---

[2] 2 Nephi 27:1
[3] Ether 4:17
[4] D&C 88:84
[5] D&C 109:60

> *". . . in the latter days . . . shall the fullness of the gospel of the Messiah come unto the Gentiles, and from the Gentiles unto the remnant of our seed." (1 Nephi 15:13)*

As in all previous dispensations, the Gospel message is first revealed to a living Prophet of God, and then spread to the rest of the children of men through an earthly organization. Joseph Smith was the Prophet, and the message that was given to all nations is a simple one: repent and prepare for the coming of Jesus Christ, the Son of God.

> *"Send forth the elders of my church unto the nations which are afar off; unto the islands of the sea; send forth unto foreign lands; call upon all nations, first upon the Gentiles, and then upon the Jews. And behold, and lo, this shall be their cry, and the voice of the Lord unto all people: Go ye forth unto the land of Zion, that the borders of my people may be enlarged, and that her stakes may be strengthened, and that Zion may go forth unto the regions round about. Yea, let the cry go forth among all people: Awake and arise and go forth to meet the Bridegroom; behold and lo, the Bridegroom cometh; go ye out to meet him. Prepare yourselves for the great day of the Lord." (D&C 133:8–10)*

The results of this early missionary effort are without question miraculous. Thousands of people not only joined the Church, but were converted to its lifelong principles. They sacrificed their homes, land, and families in order to gather to Zion to be with the Saints. Their sacrifices solidified the Saints and created a core of leadership and strength that is still felt in the Church today.

The Establishment of Zion

The establishment of The Church of Jesus Christ of Latter-day Saints also began the temporal Kingdom of God on Earth, or Zion. In Mormon doctrine, the term "Zion" has several meanings. On a personal level, Zion means the "pure in heart." In a spiritual and temporal sense,

Zion is any place in the world where the Church is established in either branches, wards, or stakes. In political terms, Zion is represented by the United States Constitution. In geographic terms, Zion is America.

It was prophesied that the Lord would raise up a mighty nation among the Gentiles on the land now called America, and it would be called Zion.[6]

> *". . . the times cometh . . . that the Lord God will raise up a mighty nation among the Gentiles, yea, even upon the face of this land." (1 Nephi 22:7)*

This great nation, the United States of America, is Zion. Joseph Smith saw the day when *all* of North America would be considered Zion. In the broadest sense, Zion could be considered any place in the world that conforms to the laws and principles embodied in the U.S. Constitution: laws that must be lived in order to form a righteous society.

> *"You know there has been great discussion in relation to Zion . . . the prophets have spoken and written upon it; but I will make a proclamation that will cover a broader ground. The whole of America is Zion itself from north to south, and is described by the Prophets, who declare that it is the Zion where the mountain of the Lord should be, and that it should be in the center of the Land." (TPJS, p. 362)*

Zion would be a land of liberty to all men (not just those who accept the gospel); it would be a beacon and ensign to the Gentiles; and it would be fortified and protected from all other nations. In fact, it was given a promise that anyone who fought against Zion would fail, and in the end, would themselves perish.[7]

> *"But behold, this land, said God, shall be a land of thine inheritance, and the Gentiles shall be blessed upon the land. And this land shall be a land of liberty unto the Gentiles, and there*

---

[6] Isaiah 2:2–5; 2 Nephi 10:19; 3 Nephi 20:22; D&C 133:12–13
[7] Isaiah 60:3–5; 1 Nephi 22:14

shall be no kings upon the land, who shall raise up unto the Gentiles. And I will fortify this land against all other nations. And he that fighteth against Zion shall perish, saith God." (2 Nephi 10:10–13)

Joseph Smith taught that the Constitution of the United States was established by God as the political and legal mechanism that would protect the Kingdom of God after it was established, and that it would be the political model for the Kingdom of God during the Millennium. Therefore, in a sense, any person that believes in the principles identified with the Constitution—capitalism (free enterprise), private property, freedom of religion, etc.—would be part of Zion. Any nation that accepted those same principles of freedom could be considered part of Zion—as long as those principles were followed by that nation and lived by its people.[8]

> *"The constitution came forth to prepare the way for the restoration of the gospel, the fulfilling of the covenants God made with ancient Israel, and the organization of the Church and Kingdom of God on earth in the last days." (Mormon Doctrine, p. 160)*

> *"But few, if any, understand what a theocratic government is. In every sense of the word, it is a republican government, and differs but little in form from our National, State, and Territorial Governments; but its subjects will recognize the will and dictation of the Almighty." (Brigham Young, Journal of Discourses, 6:342)*

The Saints have been commanded to build a great city, a "New Jerusalem," where Christ will actually dwell during the one thousand years of the millennium.[9] This great city will be the center place of Zion and is none other than the site of the original garden of Eden.

---

[8] D&C 101:80
[9] 3 Nephi 20:22

> *"In accord with the revelations given to the Prophet Joseph Smith, we teach that the Garden of Eden was on the American continent located where the City Zion, or the New Jerusalem, will be built." (Doctrines of Salvation 3:74)*

The center place of Zion, the place where the "New Jerusalem" will be built and where Christ will actually come when he returns in glory, is located in Jackson County, Missouri.[10]

> *"Hearken, O ye elders of my church, saith the Lord your God, who have assembled yourselves together, according to my commandments, in this land, which is the land of Missouri, which is the land which I have appointed and consecrated for the gathering of the saints. Wherefore, this is the land of promise, and the place for the city of Zion. And thus saith the Lord your God, if you will receive wisdom here is wisdom. Behold, the place which is now called Independence is the center place; and a spot for the temple is lying westward, upon a lot which is not far from the courthouse." (D&C 57:1–3)*

The early church was commanded to start building the city of New Jerusalem by dedicating and building a temple in Independence, Missouri. It was assumed at that time that both the temple and city would be built immediately. The Saints at that time had great hope that they would live to see the Second Coming of Christ.[11]

> *"Verily this is the word of the Lord, that the city New Jerusalem shall be built by the gathering of the saints, beginning at this place, even the place of the temple, which temple shall be reared in this generation." (D&C 84:4)*

The history and progress of the building up of Zion has been well documented in Church history and in the scriptures. The Saints were commanded to begin building the New Jerusalem in 1831. In order to participate in this great event, the Saints were required to live the Law of Consecration. This law required the Saints to enter into a covenant

---

[10] D&C 29:8; 45:63–69
[11] D&C 124:26–28

to give all of their worldly possessions to the Church and live the United Order—a society governed by Celestial laws whereby the Saints consecrated all their property and material wealth to the Church, and in return received from the Church all land, food, and material possessions they required to live and prosper. This was done by a written and legal deed and was administered to each family by the local Bishop of the Church. If the family did well with the "stewardship" they had received, they were given more. If they refused to work, or were unwise and did poorly with what they had received, they would be given less. At the end of each year, surplus goods were given to the local Bishop by each family and put into the "Bishop's Storehouse." Then, each family would be interviewed, their faithfulness assessed, and excess lands and goods redistributed to the saints according to their abilities, faithfulness, and needs. Also, the poor among the Saints were cared for out of the abundance held in the Bishop's Storehouse.

Unfortunately, this great "experiment" failed due to the greed and dishonesty of those who participated. And although the dedication of the temple site was completed by Joseph Smith, the first opportunity the saints had to start building the temple and the city of New Jerusalem was lost due to transgression.

> *"And that those who call themselves after my name might be chastened for a little season with a sore and grievous chastisement, because they did not hearken altogether unto the precepts and commandments which I gave unto them." (D&C 103:4)*

> *"Therefore, in consequence of the transgressions of my people, it is expedient in me that mine elders should wait for a little season for the redemption of Zion." (D&C 105:9)*

In hindsight, these early Saints failed to begin the temple or build the New Jerusalem because they failed to live the United Order, and were therefore deemed unworthy to participate in this sacred undertaking. In addition, the Lord placed great trials upon them, and they were forced to endure terrible persecutions at the hands of evil men.

They were driven from New York to Ohio, Missouri, Illinois, and, in the end, completely out of the United States. The early Saints were required to go through these persecutions and trials in order to chasten, purge, and purify them. Though some looked back and saw failures, others could see the broader picture as revealed to the Prophet Joseph Smith. The foundation those early Saints laid has endured, for, in reality, the existence of Zion became firmly established with the building and dedication of the first temple in Kirtland Ohio and continues to be enlarged with every new temple that is built.

The Saints are still under obligation to gather to Zion and to build the "New Jerusalem"—this commandment has simply been deferred to a future time. Since those early days of the Church of Christ, Zion has grown in power, strength, and wealth. Faithful Saints around the world await the day when the Prophet of the Church will call for a new gathering to begin, when the Saints will return to Jackson County, Missouri, live the United Order, have the privilege of building the Temple, and complete the City of New Jerusalem.

The Cleansing of Zion

It was prophesied that the United States would be punished for how they treated the Saints of God and because they rejected the Gospel. This "purging" would not only cleanse the land through the shedding of blood, but would prepare the way for the Ten Tribes of Israel to return from the North countries (of Europe).

> *"I am prepared to say by the authority of Jesus Christ, that not many years shall pass away before the United States shall present such a scene of bloodshed as has not a parallel in the history of our nation; pestilence, hail, famine, and earthquake will sweep the wicked of this generation from off the face of the land, to open and prepare the way for the return of the lost tribes of Israel from the north country." (TPJS, p. 17)*

Joseph Smith made it clear in several statements that the "Ten Tribes" in the "North Countries" meant that the Lost Tribes of Israel were scattered in the countries *north* of the land of Israel. They were not taken off of the planet (as Enoch was), nor are they hiding as a group somewhere on the earth or under the earth. They were simply scattered and "lost" among the nations of the earth and will be gathered as the Gospel spreads into each nation that has the seed of Israel among them.

> "Because the house of Israel is scattered in all nations, the gathering must take place on all the surface of the earth . . . The Ten Tribes shall return after they accept the Book of Mormon; then they shall come to Ephraim to receive their blessings, the blessings of the house of the Lord, the blessings that make them heirs of the covenant God made with their father Abraham.
>
> "But, says one, are they not in a body somewhere in the land of the north? Answer: They are not; they are scattered in all nations. The north countries of their habitation are all the countries north of their Palestinian home . . ." (Millenial Messiah, pp. 215–216)

As prophesied, the faithful Saints escaped the effects of this bloodshed by following the Prophet Brigham Young to the Rocky Mountains, which at the time was not part of the United States.

> "I prophesied that the Saints would . . . be driven to the Rocky Mountains, and some of you will live to go and assist in making settlements and build cities and see the Saints become a mighty people in the midst of the Rocky Mountains." (HC 5:85)

It was *after* the Saints fled to the Salt Lake Valley that the Civil war broke out. There was more death and bloodshed in this war than occurred in all the other U.S. wars combined. All of the faithful saints at the time were saved from participating in this war because they had followed Brigham Young to Utah. This terrible war truly fulfilled Joseph's prophesy: the wicked were punished and humbled, and the nation was prepared for the flood of people who would come in response to freedom's call.

Soon after the Civil war, a period of U.S. immigration began in which thousands of people left their homes in Europe to seek out the freedom of Zion (America). As prophesied, all who sought freedom and sought to escape the war and destruction so frequent in other countries came to Zion. It is important to keep a broad view of the prophesies concerning Zion. *All* those who came to America to seek freedom and safety fulfilled Joseph Smith's prophesy, not just those who came because of the Gospel.

Finally, remember that all of America is Zion. The United States is that nation that was prophesied to come forth in the last days; a land of liberty and freedom. It was prophesied that there would be wars in every land, but that "Zion" would be protected[12] (since the 'cleansing' of the Civil War, the United States has been, and will be, protected from her enemies). The power and stature of this nation is so great that, as prophesied, the nations of the earth fear to go to war with America. Although the time will come that the United States Government will fall, it will be due to the wickedness of its people, not because of the fear or force of other nations.

Wars and Rumors of Wars

Joseph Smith prophesied that, beginning with the Civil War (the war to cleanse Zion), war would be poured out upon all nations.[13]

> *"Verily, thus saith the Lord concerning the wars that will shortly come to pass, beginning at the rebellion of South Carolina which will eventually terminate in the death and misery of many souls; and the time will come that war will be poured out upon all nations, beginning at this place." (D&C 87:1-2)*

---

[12] See Note 2
[13] 1 Nephi 14:16–17

Almost unending war will continue until war and destruction make an end of all nations. These wars will take two forms: wars of preparation and wars of cleansing. Wars of preparation are designed to humble men and nations into accepting the Gospel of Jesus Christ. Wars of cleansing are designed to prepare the earth for the reign of the righteous. Most of these wars will consist primarily of the wicked fighting against the wicked[14] as Zion will be protected by the Lord.

> *"And thus, with the sword and by bloodshed the inhabitants of the earth shall mourn . . . until the consumption decreed hath made a full end of all nations."* (D&C 87:6)

> *"The Lord says the wicked will not repent, and because they will not repent he has decreed wars to come upon them, and the wicked shall slay the wicked, and thus the earth will be cleansed."* (Doctrines of Salvation 3:42)

The primary purpose of these wars is to cause the people of the earth to repent, receive the gospel; and bring to pass the designs of God. Just as the Civil War prepared Zion to receive the thousands of saints and emigrants seeking freedom, each new war has opened doors to new nations. This happened in two ways: first, as the political principles of Zion (the U.S. Constitution) were promoted and accepted around the world, those nations obtained the freedom of religion that permitted the Church to send in missionaries and establish branches of the Church; and second, as war decimated the countries involved, the wicked were destroyed and their poverty and need permitted both the political Zion (the United States) and the spiritual Zion (the Church) to go into those impoverished countries to meet their temporal needs, and eventually, meet their spiritual needs by teaching them the Gospel.

As the Gospel of Christ reaches the entire world, the nature of these wars will change. Instead of preparing nations to receive the Gospel, they will act as a cleansing mechanism (as the Civil War did in the United States), to prepare the world for the coming of Jesus Christ by destroying the wicked.

---

[14] 1 Nephi 22:13–14; see Note 3

11

THE TIMES OF THE JEWS (OR ISRAEL)

As prophesied, approximately one hundred years from the beginning of the Times of the Gentiles, an event or sign occurred that signaled the end of that period of missionary work and the start of the next. That event was the return of the Jews to Jerusalem and the establishment of the Nation of Israel. The formal establishment of the Nation of Israel began what is known as the *Times of the Jews*. Of course, this did not mean that the preaching of the Gospel to the Gentiles stopped, only that the emphasis of missionary work would be shifted to other nations. This shift occurred naturally. As the righteous were converted to the Gospel, or lured by the righteous principles of Zion and then physically migrated to Zion, it left those nations barren and empty. Successful missionary work would then naturally shift to other nations. That natural shift, known and prophesied ahead of time by the Lord, would now go to the Jews or Israel.

The Savior explained the timetable of missionary work in this way: the Jews were to be scattered and Jerusalem trodden down *until* the Times of the Gentiles was fulfilled.[15]

> *"And they shall fall by the edge of the sword, and shall be led away captive into all nations: and Jerusalem shall be trodden down of the Gentiles, until the times of the Gentiles be fulfilled." (Luke 21:24)*

The creation of the Nation of Israel was the most important sign to be given in the last days! The generation that witnesses the establishment of the Nation of Israel will also witness the second coming of Jesus Christ!

> *"Verily I say unto you, this generation, the generation when the times of the Gentiles be fulfilled, shall not pass away, till all be fulfilled." (Luke 21:32 JST)*

As noted before, one generation is approximately one hundred years. So it follows that sometime between 1948 (the year the Nation

---

[15] Romans 11:25; D&C 45:25, 43; see Note 4

of Israel declared its independence) and the year 2048 the Lord will come to set up an earthly Kingdom that will create one thousand years of peace.

In 1836, Joseph Smith prophesied that Jerusalem would be redeemed from that very hour, and that the Jews would begin their return. He later sent Apostle Orson Hyde to Jerusalem to dedicate the land for the return of the Jews. As prophesied, it would not be the Jews who accomplished this feat, but the Gentiles. History shows that as early as 1840, leaders in prominent positions in Europe and the United States were developing plans—and using political means—to bring the Jews back to Palestine.

It had been prophesied that it would be the Gentiles, the sons of strangers, who would save and restore Israel—Gentiles who would build up their walls—and it would be the wealth of the Gentile Nations that would flow into Israel to help her exist.[16]

In the history book, *The Bible and Sword* by Barbara Tuchman (p. 175), she provides specific details of some of the actions that were taken by Gentile Nations to bring this great event about. These are just a few examples of actions taken by political figures in Gentile Nations that covered a hundred years of effort:

> "There exists at the present time among the Jews dispersed over Europe, a strong notion that the time is approaching when their nation is to return to Palestine . . . It would be of manifest importance to the Sultan to encourage the Jews to return and to settle in Palestine because of the wealth which they would bring with them . . . I have to instruct Your Excellency strongly to recommend (the Turkish government) to hold out every just encouragement to the Jews of Europe to return to Palestine." (August 11, 1840, Lord Shaftesbury of England)
>
> "On August 17 the Times of London published a leader on a plan 'to plant the Jewish people in the land of their fathers,'

---

[16] Ezekiel 36:24

which, it said, was now under 'serious political consideration.'
It commended the efforts . . . as 'practical and statesmanlike.' "

Knowledge of the fulfillment of this prophesy can even be found in our encyclopedias. It lists these events as common knowledge:

> *"A combination of factors made possible the emergence of this unique state. (1) The Zionist movement, which developed toward the end of the 19th Century. (2) The Balfour Declaration of 1917, by which the British Government undertook to aid the creation of a national home for the Jews in Palestine. (3) Under the mandate for Palestine given to Britain by the League of Nations in 1922, the Yishuv (the Jewish settlement before statehood) developed the foundations of its national institutions. (4) In November 1947, the United Nations called for the partition of Palestine into separate Jewish and Arab states. (5) In May 1948, the Jews declared the independence of the State of Israel, and fought a brief, but intense war with its Arab neighbors to secure their new state."* (Encyclopedia Americana 1990, *Vol. 15, p. 520*)

These actions by other Nations to bring about the existence of the Nation of Israel is commonly known. Many "Gentile Nations" worked for years to bring about the actual, physical return of the Jewish Nation to their ancient homeland. History clearly shows that the Jews themselves had little to do with this great event. The Jewish Nation was brought about by—and continues to be sustained by—the wealth and support of "Gentile" Nations. This momentous event had been prophesied for over 2,000 years, and is one of the greatest signs signaling the coming of Jesus Christ.

> *"Thus saith the Lord God, behold, I will lift up mine hand to the Gentiles, and set up my standard to the people: and they shall bring thy sons in their arms, and thy daughters shall be carried upon their shoulders."* (Isaiah 49:22)

> *"Then thou shalt see . . . the wealth of the Gentiles shall come unto thee. And the sons of strangers shall build up thy walls and their kings shall minister unto thee. Thou shalt suck the*

milk of the Gentiles, and shalt suck the breast of
kings." (Isaiah 60:5, 10, 16)

Israel's possession of nuclear weapons has made them the third most powerful nation in the world (after the U.S.A. and Russia). Their peculiar religion and their political and national presence has continued to make them a thorn in the side of many nations, and will eventually make them the focal point of the final war—the war of Armageddon.[17]

This period of missionary work was not only to try to convert the Jews, but to seek out all of the Tribes of Israel. And although there has been some success among the Jews (there has been a strong branch of the Church in Israel for many years), the greatest work of this period has been among the Tribe of Manasseh, or the Lamanites, living in Central and South America. The great Jewish conversion will come when the Savior himself returns to Jerusalem. But the Lamanites have entered the Church by the millions. Almost half the total membership of the Church is now represented by the descendants of Lehi.

THE TIMES OF THE HEATHEN NATIONS

It was prophesied that the last people to hear the Gospel would be the Heathen Nations, or the nations of the earth descended from Cain and Ham (these nations were commonly called the "Heathen Nations" in the scriptures).

> *"That through your administration . . . the word may go forth*
> *unto the ends of the earth, unto the Gentiles first, and then*
> *they shall turn unto the Jews. And then cometh the day when*
> *the arm of the Lord shall be revealed in power in convincing*
> *the heathen nations of the gospel of their salvation." (D&C*
> *90:9–10)*

---

[17] Isaiah 19:16–17

15

The reason the Heathen Nations are to be the last to hear and receive the full blessings of the Gospel is due to the curse placed upon the descendants of Cain and Ham after they transgressed the commandments of God. The curse was that Cain and his descendants would be denied the privilege of being ordained to the Priesthood of God. In order that men might know *who* the descendants of Cain and Ham were, God placed "a mark" of a dark skin upon them.[18]

> *"And the Lord set a mark upon Cain, lest any finding him should kill him." (Genesis 4:15)*

> *"Now this king of Egypt was a descendant from the loins of Ham, and was a partaker of the blood of the Canaanites by birth. From this descent sprang all the Egyptians, and thus the blood of the Canaanites was preserved in the land. The land of Egypt being first discovered by a woman, who was the daughter of Ham, and the daughter of Egyptus, which signifies that which is forbidden; and thus, from Ham, sprang that race which preserved the curse in the land." (Abraham 1:21–24)*

> *"Now, Pharaoh being of that lineage by which he could not have the right of Priesthood, notwithstanding the Pharaohs would fain claim it from Noah through Ham." (Abraham 1:27)*

As difficult as it may be for the descendants of Cain and Ham to accept the knowledge and reality of the curse—and the reasons for it—it is clear they would be the last race of people upon the face of the earth to receive the full blessings of the Gospel.

> *"The first man that committed the odious crime of killing one of his brethren will be cursed the longest of any one of the children of Adam. Cain slew his brother . . . and the Lord put a mark upon him . . . How long is that race to endure the dreadful curse that is upon them? That curse will remain upon them, and they never can hold the Priesthood or share in it until all the other descendants of Adam have received the*

---

[18] Genesis 4:25–26, 9:8; Moses 7:8, 22

promises and enjoyed the blessings of the Priesthood and the
keys thereof. They were the first that were cursed, and they
will be the last from whom the curse will be removed."
(Brigham Young, Journal of Discourses, 7:290)

We have also been told that other nations (such as India and China) have been similarly cursed, and are also considered "Heathen Nations" (though we do not know how or why they became cursed). And as "Heathen Nations," they will be part of this last missionary effort before the coming of the Lord.

"The great nation of China is a heathen Nation. I do not expect to see great numbers of people join the Church in such lands, but the obligation is upon us to carry the news to them, for it must go to all flesh, whether they receive it or not; and whosoever shall receive it shall find the full salvation of God . . . and this obligation I say is yet resting upon the Elders of this Church." (Melvin J. Ballard, Conference Report April 1925, p. 132)

In 1978, a few years after the first branch of the Church was established in Israel, the Prophet Spencer W. Kimball received a revelation concerning the Priesthood. It was revealed that the time had come for the curse to be lifted, and that all worthy people (including the Heathen Nations) could receive the Priesthood and all of the blessings that come from the Temple. This event, or sign, ended the Times of the Jews, and began the *Times of the Heathen Nations*. The command to preach the Gospel to all the world was now in its last stage.

We are now living in that last period of missionary work. During this time, missionaries are flooding Africa and Asia, as well as continuing to proselyte the rest of the world. Soon China and India will fully open their doors and the gospel will truly have gone to all the earth. Just as anciently on the American continent, prior to the visit of Jesus Christ, there will be a short period of time when the entire earth will be at peace and open to missionary work. The political principles of Zion (the U.S. Constitution) will be accepted worldwide, and will permit free trade and open borders between all countries. However, this era of freedom will end quickly, just as it did among the ancient Nephites.

> "And behold, there was peace in all the land, insomuch that the Nephites did go into whatsoever part of the land they would...and it came to pass that the Lamanites did also go withersoever they would, whether it were among the Lamanites or the Nephites; and thus they did have free intercourse one with another, to buy and to sell, and to get gain, according to their desire. And it came to pass that they became exceedingly rich, both the Lamanites and the Nephites." (Helaman 6:7–9)

And just as happened with the Nephites prior to the coming of Christ, the Church will grow in power and influence until it covers the whole earth.

> "And so great was the prosperity of the church, and so many the blessings which were poured out upon the people, that even the high priests and the teachers were themselves astonished beyond measure." (Helaman 3:25)

Solomon's Temple Rebuilt

Prior to the Second Coming of Jesus Christ, two temples must be built: the temple in the center of the New Jerusalem (in America), and the rebuilding of Solomon's Temple (in Jerusalem).

> "Judah must return, Jerusalem must be rebuilt, and the temple . . . It will take some time to rebuild the walls of the city and the temple, and all this must be done before the Son of Man will make his appearance." (TPJS p. 286)

The Jerusalem Temple will be constructed under the direction of The Church of Jesus Christ of Latter-day Saints, as they are the only authorized servants of God in the last days.

> "And they that are far off shall come and build in the Temple of the Lord." (Zechariah 6:12–15)

> *"Who are those 'that are far off' who shall come to Jerusalem to build the house of the Lord? Surely they are the Jews who have been scattered afar. By what power and under whose authorization shall the work be done? There is only one people who know how to build temples and what to do in them when they are completed. That people is the Latter-day Saints."*
> (Millenial Messiah, p. 279)

After the temple in Jerusalem is rebuilt, the prophesy concerning a restoration of animal sacrifice will take place. As the Jews reclaim their rights as the chosen people of God and begin to reestablish the ancient traditions, the practice of sacrificing animals will be restored. The Jews are still the rightful heirs of the Aaronic Priesthood, and it will be at this time that they will claim their right to perform all of the ancient rituals and ceremonies, including the sacrifice of animals (a symbol of the sacrifice of Jesus Christ).

> *"To complete the restoration of all things . . . sacrifices will again be offered in this dispensation. John the Baptist, for instance, brought back the commission and power whereby the sons of Levi shall offer again in righteousness those offerings which they made in ancient days. (D&C 13)"* (Mormon Doctrine, p. 666, "Sacrifices")

> *"The offering of sacrifice has ever been connected and forms a part of the duties of the priesthood. It began with the priesthood, and will be continued until after the coming of Christ, from generation to generation. These sacrifices, as well as every ordinance belonging to the priesthood, will, when the Temple of the Lord shall be built, and the sons of Levi be purified, be fully restored and attended to in all their powers, ramifications, and blessings."* (TPJS, pp. 172–173)

The events leading to the building and dedication of Solomon's Temple may be the catalyst that will make Jerusalem the focal point of the final war.

NOTES

1. Joseph Fielding Smith, *Doctrines of Salvation* Vol. 3:3-5.
    "WARNING VOICE ALWAYS PRECEDES JUDGMENTS. Would it not be an extraordinarily strange thing if the Lord should come and begin his reign of peace—take vengeance on the wicked, cleanse the earth from sin—and not send messengers to prepare the way before him? Should we expect the Lord to come to judge the world without first giving it warning and preparing the means of escape for all who will repent?
    "The implication in these words of our Lord—that 'this gospel of the kingdom shall be preached in all the world for a witness unto all nations; and then shall the end come'—the implication is that in the last days the Lord would give as a sign to all nations the sending anew of the message of the gospel of the kingdom and that it would be different from the teachings then being taught and received among the nations. Otherwise how could it be distinguished and accepted as a sign of his second coming? Moreover, when this declaration of the gospel of the kingdom should reach all nations, then should the end come, or in other words, the time for the appearance of our Lord."

2. *Teachings of the Prophet Joseph Smith*, Section 4:161.
    "No Peace But in Zion" . . . The time is soon coming, when no man will have any peace but in Zion and her stakes . . . I saw men hunting the lives of their own sons, and brother murdering brother, women killing their own daughters, and daughters seeking the lives of their mothers. I saw armies arrayed against armies. I saw blood, desolation, fires. The Son of man has said that the mother shall be against the daughters, and the daughter against the mother. These things are at our doors."

3. Joseph Fielding Smith, *Doctrines of Salvation*, Vol. 3:42–43.
    "WICKED TO SLAY WICKED UNTIL THE LORD COMES. The Lord says he has decreed wars. Why? Because of the hatred in the hearts of men, because of the wickedness in the hearts of men, because they will not repent. Here is another passage: 'And it shall come to pass, because of the wickedness of the world, that I will take vengeance upon the wicked, for they will not repent; for the cup of mine indignation is full; for behold, my blood shall not cleanse them if they hear me not.' These things the Lord said through his Prophet in warnings that have come to the people of this nation and other lands. The Lord says the wicked will not repent, and because they will not repent he has decreed wars to come upon them, and the wicked shall slay the wicked, and thus the earth will be cleansed, as we read in the 24th chapter of Isaiah, until there shall be few men left."

4. Joseph Fielding Smith, *Doctrines of Salvation,* Vol. 3:8.

"TIMES OF GENTILES TO BE FULFILLED. We go unto them with a message of peace, of truth, of eternal salvation, calling upon them to repent of their sins and enter into the true fold, where they may receive rest. When they will not do this, but to the contrary, will listen to the unrighteous and condemn the truth, then God will withdraw the gospel from among them. In that day the times of the Gentiles will be fulfilled and the gospel will be carried to the Jews."

Chapter Two
The Anti-Christ

Some time soon, perhaps as a result of the rebuilding of the temple in Jerusalem, a man will come to power that will use deception and lies to build a coalition of ten nations. Once his power is consolidated, he will begin a war of conquest that will eventually end in his control of most of the world. He will persecute the Saints, and will seek to destroy the Jews.[1] The reason for his popularity will be, first, his ability to make the economies of the world and individuals prosperous, and second, his weapons of war and ability to destroy all who oppose him. The real source of his power will come from a covenant he has made with Satan. In the end he will destroy Jerusalem and place his throne in the newly rebuilt Temple, desecrating it. *Then he will challenge Jesus Christ himself for control of the earth.*

> *"Let no man deceive you by any means . . . for that day shall not come, except there come a falling away first, and that man of sin be revealed, the son of perdition; who opposeth and exalteth himself above all that is called God, or that is worshiped; so that he as God sitteth in the temple of God, showing himself that he is God." (2 Thessalonians 2:3–4)*

---

[1] 2 Thessalonians 2:7–9 JST; Revelation 9:11, 19:19

> *"And in the latter time of their kingdom, when the transgressors are come to the full, a king of fierce countenance, and understanding dark sentences, shall stand up. And his power shall be mighty, but not by his own power; and he shall destroy wonderfully, and shall prosper, and practice, and shall destroy the mighty and the holy people. And through his policy also he shall cause craft to prosper in his hand; and he shall magnify himself to his heart, and in a time of peace shall destroy many; he shall also stand up against the Prince of princes; but he shall be broken without hand." (Daniel 8:23–25)*

After the Anti-Christ comes to power, he will persuade ten nations to form an alliance or coalition, then they will go to war. To create this unholy alliance he will send out three men—"false prophets" who will use deception and false miracles to convince the people of these ten nations to join in a war for world domination. This will be a long war, resulting in the death of one-third of all people living at the time, and culminating in one great final battle: the "Battle of Armageddon."

> *"And the ten horns which thou sawest are ten kings, which have received no kingdom as yet; but receive power as kings one hour with the beast." (Revelation 17:12)*

> *"And I saw three unclean spirits come out of the mouth of the dragon. For they are the spirits of devils, working miracles, which go forth unto the kings of the earth and of the whole world, to gather them to the battle of that great day of God Almighty. And he gathered them together into a place called in the Hebrew tongue Armageddon." (Revelation 16:13–16)*

Due to the wickedness existing in the world, the Anti-Christ will easily prevail against all other nations and reap destruction upon the Saints of God as they attempt to flee to the safety of Zion. He will have continuous success in this war of death and destruction *until* the Ancient of Days (Adam) comes, and Christ receives the keys of the kingdom at Adam-ondi-Ahman.

24

" . . . and the same horn made war with the saints, and prevailed against them; until the Ancient of days came, and judgment was given to the saints of the most high; and the time
came that the saints possessed the kingdom. Thus he said, the
fourth beast shall be diverse from all kingdoms, and shall de-
vour the whole earth, and shall tread it down, and break it in
pieces. And the ten horns out of this kingdom are ten kings
that shall arise, and another shall arise after them. And he
shall speak great words against the most high, and shall wear
out the saints of the most high, and think to change times and
laws." (Daniel 7:19–25)

THE WORLD REJECTS THE GOSPEL AND
ALL MISSIONARIES ARE CALLED HOME

One of the effects the Anti-Christ will have upon the nations of
the earth will be a complete separation of the wicked and the righteous. Just as in past wars, this separation will begin because of a flood
of propaganda against the Saints. The lies sent out by the Anti-Christ
will become so accepted that people will no longer believe and accept
the Gospel when preached. As propaganda turns to actions, the persecution of the Saints and the Jews will begin in earnest. This persecution will result in the decision to call all missionaries home to Zion.
Then even the Saints will be commanded to gather to Zion. As the
Anti-Christ moves from one nation to the next, the righteous will flee
before him.[2]

"All we have yet heard and all we have experienced is scarcely
a preface to the sermon that is going to be preached. When the
testimony of the Elders ceases to be given, and the Lord says to
them, 'come home; I will now preach my own sermons to the
nations of the earth.' " (Brigham Young, Journal of Discourses, 8:123)

---

[2] D&C 45:26–27; 2 Nephi 27:1

25

> *"These missionaries and labourers are now called home. The Lord says, 'It is enough. Come out of her, my people,' is now the voice of God to his servants in every land and nation. The vials of his wrath cannot be poured out until you, like Lot, flee from the countries doomed to feel the vengeance of God." (Orson Pratt, Journal of Discourses, 6:15)*

After the missionaries are called home, the "testimony of disasters" will begin: the world will hear God himself speak to them through three powerful events (see *Testimony of Disasters*, Chapter 4).

THE UNITED STATES GOVERNMENT FALLS

Even Zion (America), though protected by covenant from destruction by other nations, even Zion will be full of wickedness, and will eventually collapse into lawless anarchy.[3] At that critical time, with the constitution hanging by a thread. The Church of Jesus Christ of Latter-day Saints will step forward, reestablish order out of chaos, and begin to build the New Jerusalem to prepare for the coming of Christ.

> *". . . every government in the world, including the United States, will have to become part of the government of God. Then righteous rule will be established. The earth will be cleansed; the wicked will be destroyed; and the reign of peace will be ushered in." (Doctrines of Salvation 3:13)*

> *"Will the Constitution be destroyed? No: it will be held inviolate by this people; and, as Joseph Smith said, 'The time will come when the destiny of the nation will hang upon a single thread. At that critical juncture, this people will step forth and save it from the threatened destruction.' It will be so." (Brigham Young, Journal of Discourses, 7:15)*

As the Anti-Christ gathers the wicked and destroys the nations and governments of the earth, the righteous will continue to be gathered to

---

[3] See Note 1

Zion—to build the New Jerusalem, establish the government and Kingdom of God, and prepare to receive Christ. This process will continue until there is a complete separation of the righteous and the wicked. When the wheat and the tares are fully separated, the Angels of God will reap destruction upon the earth.

Notes

1. Orson Pratt, *Journal of Discourses,* 13:126.
"The great nation of the United States, one of the best governments ever organized by human authority on the earth, must pass away in many of its features . . . then all the great and glorious principles incorporated in this great republic will be incorporated in the kingdom of God and be preserved."

Orson Pratt, *Journal of Discourses,* 20:151.
"The war that destroyed the lives of some 5 or 6 hundred thousand people (the Civil War) was nothing compared to that which will eventually devastate that country (America). It will be very different from the war between the North and the South. It will be a war of neighborhood against neighborhood, city against city, state against state, and they will go forth destroying and being destroyed . . . that great nation will be wasted away, unless they repent."

Chapter Three
The New Jerusalem

As the war of the Anti-Christ rages around the world and persecution descends upon both the Saints and the Jews, the time will come that the Prophet of the Church sends out the call to gather to the New Jerusalem.

At first, the center place of Zion (Jackson County, Missouri) is repurchased quietly. As the Church grows in size and wealth, more land is purchased until the day comes that the Church owns not only the land for the building of the city of New Jerusalem, but a good portion of America as well (this process has already been going on for some time, and members of the Church would be stunned to know how much property and businesses the Church owns and operates).

> Not many years hence you will look forth to the western counties of the State of Missouri, and you will see a thickly populated country, inhabited by a peaceful people — the Latter-day Saints. They have come from the nations of the earth . . . and from the North American continent. And when we purchase the land, and take possession of it, I do not think we will be driven from our own lands. When the time comes for purchasing this land, we will have the means. I will here prophesy . . . there are no people now upon the face of the earth, so rich as the Latter-day Saints will be in a few years to come. Having their millions; therefore they will purchase the land, build up

> cities, towns and villages, build a great capital city, at head-
> quarters, in Jackson County, Missouri." (Orson Pratt, Jour-
> nal of Discourses, 21:135)

As the Saints gather from around the world, they come to a land of America that is falling apart. The laws that once created the greatest nation in the history of the known world have been corrupted by evil men, and have led a once righteous people to the very brink of economic and political collapse. The United States government is ineffective and overwhelmed by the wickedness of the people. So many laws are broken that prisons cannot hold them, and the police are impotent in the general anarchy. Street gangs rule the cities, as vigilante groups try to keep a semblance of order in the suburbs. Just as with the government of the Nephites, the Constitution—along with the U.S. government—has been so corrupted that it cannot be recognized, and cannot help the people it was designed to protect.

> " . . . they had altered and trampled under their feet the laws
> of Mosiah, or that which the Lord commanded him to give
> unto the people; and they saw that their laws had become cor-
> rupted, and that they had become a wicked people . . . and
> because of their iniquity the church had begun to dwindle;
> and they began to disbelieve in the spirit of prophecy and in
> the spirit of revelation; and the judgments of God did stare
> them in the face. And they saw that they had become
> weak . . . and that the spirit of the Lord did no more preserve
> them . . . And thus had they fallen into this great transgres-
> sion; yea, thus had they become weak, because of their trans-
> gression, in the space of not many years (8 years)." (Helaman
> 4:22–26)

> "For as their laws and their governments were established by
> the voice of the people, and they who chose evil were more
> numerous than they who chose good, therefore they were rip-
> ening for destruction, for the laws had become corrupted."
> (Helaman 5:2)

Amid this scene of chaos and fear, a bright light shines: The Church of Jesus Christ of Latter-day Saints. The Church has become a beacon of light in a black sea of corruption. Totally independent due to its wealth and worldwide organization, the Church becomes a government within a government. Its armies of faithful priesthood holders and its financial empire gives the Church an influence and power that sets it above all other organizations and nations on earth.

As the Saints gather from around the world to Zion, great sacrifices must be made. The Saints are required to consecrate all their worldly goods to the Church. They are then given a place to live and work to do. Anyone refusing to work does not eat. Anyone refusing to consecrate their material goods and strictly obey the laws that have been established are not permitted to live within the Society. The Church will have created their own police force and militia to protect Zion. The laws are very strict, and the punishment for breaking any law is immediate. But there is peace and prosperity.[1]

The return of the Saints to Zion, and specifically their return to the center place of Zion to start building the New Jerusalem, will be much like the exodus of the ancient Israelites. After the call comes from the Prophet of God to gather, large groups of Saints will be led by the hand of the Lord to their new home in Zion. During their journey they will be protected from the evil and chaos seeking to prevent them from reaching their destination. Miracles will happen in view of all.[2]

> "I expect that when the Lord leads forth his people to build up the city of Zion, his presence will be visible. When we speak of the presence of the Lord we speak of an exhibition of power. We shall go back to Jackson County. When we go back there will be a very large organization consisting of thousands, and tens of thousands, and they will march forward, the glory of God overshadowing their camp by day in the form of a cloud, and a pillar of flaming fire by night, the

---

[1] D&C 49:25
[2] D&C 101:18, 133:26–35; Moses 7:62

> *Lord's voice being uttered forth before his army. The ever-*
> *lasting hills will rejoice, and they will tremble before the*
> *presence of the Lord; and his people will go forth and build*
> *up Zion according to celestial law." (Orson Pratt,* Journal
> of Discourses, *15:364)*

The great wealth and power of the Church will be tested as the
Anti-Christ comes to power and the Church moves to become an independent government. The Church's resources will be drained by the
flood of Saints gathering to America—many of whom will have lost
everything due to the persecution of the Anti-Christ—and the Church
is *forced* to adopt the Law of Consecration and actually live the United
Order.

> *"Unless we are equal in earthly things, we cannot be made*
> *equal in heavenly things. The Lord has told us, that it is re-*
> *quired of every man in this Church to lay all things, not one*
> *tenth alone, but to lay all things before the Bishop of His*
> *Church; consecrate the whole of it – and, it has to be conse-*
> *crated too, says the revelation, with a covenant and a (legal)*
> *deed that cannot be broken. What is the next step to be taken*
> *in order to bring about equality of property? The Lord says,*
> *'Let the Bishop appoint every man his stewardship,' for says*
> *the Lord, 'It is required of every man to render an account of*
> *his stewardship, both in time and in eternity.' But in regard*
> *to these stewardships, it is not needful or necessary, or the*
> *Lord never intended, that every man should possess an equal*
> *amount of stewardship with his brother. Why? Because God*
> *has given to some men greater ability to manage and control*
> *property than others. And if a man undertakes to squander*
> *the stewardship which the Lord has entrusted to him, He*
> *takes it away, and gives it to another who is a more wise*
> *steward; one who will manage His property in such a way as*
> *to benefit the whole; each one seeking the interest of the*
> *whole as well as of himself. If the whole Church were to con-*
> *secrate in this way they would have nothing left of their own.*
> *Then, it would all be the Lord's. And, if each one in the*
> *Church possesses the whole of it, as joint heirs with the Lord,*
> *is there not an equality?" (Orson Pratt,* Journal of Dis-
> courses, *2:98)*

The Saints will gather to Zion, both for protection and to prepare themselves for the second coming of Christ. Part of this preparation will be the need to sanctify themselves through the Law of Sacrifice. As noted above, part of that process will be the requirement to live the Law of Consecration. In addition, as noted previously, the Lord requires all who participate in the building of the New Jerusalem to live this law.

> "Wherefore, prepare ye, prepare ye, O my people; sanctify yourselves; gather ye together, O ye people of my church, upon the land of Zion, all you that have not been commanded to tarry." (D&C 133:4)

> "The object of this last dispensation is to make the people one as the Father and the Son are one, to make them 'equal in earthly things, that they may be made equal in heavenly things.' The Lord has told us — 'Let these laws I have given concerning my people in Jackson County be fulfilled after the redemption of Zion.'" (Orson Pratt, Journal of Discourses, 2:57)

After the Saints begin to gather, and prior to the Coming of Jesus Christ, they will complete the building of a new temple in the center of the New Jerusalem. It will be after this great temple is completed that Christ will come in glory to rule on earth.

> "The coming of Christ seems to be near at hand, yet Zion must be redeemed before that day; the temple must be built upon the consecrated spot, the cloud and glory of the Lord rest upon it, and the Lamanites brought in, and they must build up the New Jerusalem!" (Orson Pratt, Journal of Discourses, 3:18)

The temple will be the largest building in the city. From the few accounts we have of people who have seen this temple in vision, it will be very unique. It will consist of twelve buildings surrounding a central dome, like spokes on a wheel. Each of these separate buildings will be as large as what our largest temples are today. Each of these buildings will have a tower on its outside end, and be connected to the central core or dome at its inside end. The central dome will be massive, and exceed in size and height the twelve buildings and towers that surround it. It will be the Holy of Holies, the throne of God, and the seat of the Government of God during the Millennium.

> *"The scenery gradually changed, and a temple very much larger in dimensions than the one which we are building stood before me. There were a number of towers, placed apparently at equal distances on the outside, each of which were supported by buildings as large as this temple, and yet were united with, and were a part of the great temple. They were of as large dimensions as that which is on this temple. From the midst of these towers and in the center of the building arose in majestic grandeur an immense, large dome that seemed to tower as high above the towers as the towers were from the earth."* (Dean Jessee, The John Taylor Journal)

> *"I beheld an immense city, extending on all sides and thronged by myriads of people, apparently of all nations. In the midst of this city stood a magnificent temple, which, in magnitude and splendor, exceeded everything of the kind known upon the earth. Its foundations were of precious stones; its walls like polished gold; its windows of agates, clear as crystal; and its roof of a dazzling brightness, its top, like the lofty Andes, seemed to mingle with the skies; while a bright cloud overshadowed it, from which extended rays of glory and brightness in all the magnificent colors of the rainbow. The whole buildings thereof seemed to cover some eight or ten acres of ground. 'This' said the Angel of the Praries, 'is the sanctuary of freedom, the palace of the great King, and the center of a universal government.'"* (Parley Pratt, The Angel of the Prairies, 11–21)

Who can comprehend the sight? A glorious temple, a magnificent city, the focus of the New World, the center of the Kingdom of God on earth, and the throne of Jesus Christ. The God of Israel Himself will be there. The glory of God, of the temple, and the light of the city itself, will shine for all the world to see.

> *"The presence of the Lord will be in their midst, and it will radiate over their temples, it will light their city by night and by day. It will be a standing miracle by day and by night, until one thousand years shall have rolled away over the heads of the people that dwell on the earth. The light will shine so conspicuously from that city, extending to the very heavens, that it will in reality be like unto a city set upon a hill that cannot be hid, and it will have a tendency to strike terror to all the nations of the earth. The shining light will be seen for many miles distant, and the wicked will flee away."* (Orson Pratt, Journal of Discourses, 17:330)

This is a time of preparation for the Saints. They must prepare to receive the Lord and the glorified, resurrected Saints and angels that will come "in glory" with Him. Over time, the Saints will become prepared, both spiritually and temporally, to endure the glorified presence of the Lord and those that come with Him.

It will be here, in the city of New Jerusalem, that the Lord will come in glory when He returns to reign upon the earth. This will be *after* the great meeting at Adam-Ondi-Ahman where Christ will accept the Keys of Authority from those earthly men who hold them.

It will be in this place and during this time period that Christ will set apart 144,000 high priests to act as teachers and missionaries to lead the Saints to the "Church of the Firstborn." The Saints will be taught by these 144,000 high priests in the Temples of God *how* to make their Calling and Election sure, or be sealed into the Kingdom of God. Then the Saints will be sanctified and actually sealed to the highest degree of the Celestial Kingdom of God.

Finally, it is here that the armies of the Lord will be set apart and trained to prepare for the great confrontation with the Anti-Christ. All of this will take place during the time period *between* the meeting at Adam-ondi-Ahman and Christ's coming in glory. As all of this will take some time, Christ will actually be dwelling on earth for a long time before he comes in glory, and before going to Jerusalem to confront the Anti-Christ.

> "Zion will be favored with the presence of the Lord before the Jews are permitted to behold him. The Lord will come to the Temple of Zion before he comes to the Temple in Jerusalem. Before he comes in the clouds of heaven with power and great glory, he will manifest himself in the city and Temple of Zion; the Lord will reveal his face unto them, they will see him and he will dwell in the midst of Zion. His throne will be there. After he has come to Zion, and dwelt in their midst for a long space of time, he then goes with all his Saints to visit old Jerusalem, the last work before the day of rest shall come." (Orson Pratt, Journal of Discourses, 15:338)

ADAM-ONDI-AHMAN

This is a description of the site:[3]

> "Not long after the Prophet first visited the land of Missouri, he began receiving revelations concerning the historical importance of this area of land where Adam first lived. The land was still very beautiful, and significant landmarks were still present.

> "The Prophet designated the land at Independence and beyond as 'the land where Adam dwelt.' Further, he declared, that Spring Hill, Davies County, Missouri, is 'the place where Adam shall come to visit his people,' and called it Adam-ondi-Ahman. It is located on the north side of Grand River, on an elevated spot of ground overlooking the river and country roundabout. On the top of the hill was an ancient stone altar.

> "According to several revealed statements Adam lived in America. The Garden of Eden must then have been on the American continent. The relative location of Independence and that of Adam-ondi-Ahman corroborate the Bible. After the so-called 'Fall,' Adam and Eve were driven out of the

---

[3] See Note 1

garden and a flaming sword 'placed at the east to keep the way of the tree of life. Now Adam-ondi-Ahman is about seventy miles northeast of the city of Independence. If our first progenitors settled at Adam-ondi-Ahman, it is more likely that the people as they increased settled along the course of the Mississippi basin. Noah probably built the Ark near the river. When the flood came, it floated easily into the ocean, to the Asiatic continent where Noah and his family began again the work commenced by Adam.' " (John A. Widtsoe, **Evidences & Reconciliations**)

"The Prophet Joseph called upon Brigham, myself and others, saying, 'Brethren, come go along with me, and I will show you something.' He led us a short distance to a place where were the ruins of three altars built of stone, one above the other, and the one standing a little back of the other, like unto the pulpits in the Kirtland Temple, representing the order of three grades of Priesthood; 'There,' said Joseph, 'is the place where Adam offered up sacrifice after he was cast out of the garden.' The altar stood at the highest point of the bluff." (Heber C. Kimball, **Life of Heber C. Kimball**, p. 209)

Sometime after the City of New Jerusalem begins to be built, a sacred meeting will be held in Missouri. This event will signal the coming of the Lord Jesus Christ to the earth. He will *not* be in glory—that will come much later—but it will be the coming the Saints are waiting for.

The purpose of this meeting will be to return the keys of authority to Jesus Christ. It is a well known doctrine that during Christ's absence he gave authority to his Prophets and Apostles to build up the Kingdom of God on earth. Adam, the first man and first priesthood holder on earth, was given dominion over all the earth, and over all of his progenitors. This authority was given under the direction of Jesus Christ. Since then, all priesthood labor upon the earth has been under the authority and the direction of Adam, the first man, the Ancient of

Days. Since the keys of authority were given to men on earth by Jesus Christ, Christ will be required to reclaim those same keys from those in authority on earth at the time of his coming. This step must be taken by Christ *prior* to beginning his reign on earth. Much like a change of callings that happens in the Church twice a year at General Conference, *the Saints will witness the release of the living Prophet as the head of the Church, and be privileged to sustain Jesus Christ as the new head of the Church and Kingdom of God on earth.*

The Prophet Joseph Smith often taught about the hierarchy of the heavens, and that it is Adam, not Jesus Christ, who is our first line of authority on earth. This doctrine has often been called the Adam-God theory. The basic concept is this: Since Jesus delegated to Adam the authority to "oversee" or have "dominion" over the earth and all those who dwell on it, in this sense (and this sense only), Adam is our "God," or the first in our line of authority.

> "*The Priesthood was first given to Adam; he obtained the First Presidency, and held the keys of it from generation to generation. The keys (of the priesthood) have to be brought from heaven whenever the Gospel is sent. When they are re-vealed from heaven, it is by Adam's authority. Daniel speaks of the Ancient of Days; he means the oldest man, our Father Adam. He is the father of the human family, and presides over the spirits of all men, and all that have had the keys must stand before him in this grand council. The Son of Man stands before him, and there is given him glory and domin-ion. Adam delivers up his stewardship to Christ, that which was delivered to him as holding the keys of the universe, but retains his standing as head of the human family.*" (TPJS, p. 157)

The position of Adam as God of his posterity and the one in authority over the earth while Jesus Christ is absent presents a legal problem for the return of Jesus Christ. In order to legally and lawfully take Adam's place as ruler of the earth, Christ must return, openly make this change of office, and be sustained by all those over whom he will rule. Millions of faithful Saints will have the opportunity to witness and participate in this great event. In fact, all righteous Saints alive and dead will witness and participate in this great spiritual feast.

> *"I beheld till the thrones were set up, and the Ancient of days did sit, whose garment was white as snow, and the hair of his head like the pure wool: his throne was like the fiery flame, and his wheels as burning fire. A fiery stream issued and came forth from before him: thousand thousands ministered unto him, and ten thousand times ten thousands stood before him: the judgment was set, and the books were opened. I saw in the night visions, and, behold, one like the Son of man came with the clouds of heaven, and came to the Ancient of days, and they brought him near before him. And there was given him dominion, and glory, and a kingdom, that all people, nations, and languages, should serve him: his dominion is an everlasting dominion, which shall not pass away, and his kingdom that which shall not be destroyed." (Daniel 7:9–14)*

> *". . . Father Adam, the Ancient of Days and father of all." (D&C 138:38)*

Just like Daniel of old, Joseph Smith saw this great event, and while on a trip to Missouri it was revealed to him the very place where it would happen.

> *"Spring Hill is named by the Lord Adam-ondi-Ahman, because, said he, it is the place where Adam shall come to visit his people, or the Ancient of Days shall sit, as spoken of by Daniel the prophet." (D&C 116)*

This grand meeting will be similar in many ways to the first meeting at Adam-ondi-Ahman conducted by Adam, just prior to his death. As noted above, this future meeting will take place on the same spot as the previous meeting of Saints in the time of Adam.

> *"Three years previous to the death of Adam, he called . . . his posterity who were righteous, into the valley of Adam-ondi-ahman, and there bestowed upon them his last blessing. And the Lord appeared unto them, and they rose up and blessed*

> *Adam, and called him Michael, the prince, the archangel.*
> *And Adam stood up in the midst of the congregation; and,*
> *notwithstanding he was bowed down with age, being full of*
> *the Holy Ghost, predicted whatsoever should befall his pos-*
> *terity unto the latest generation." (D&C 107:53–57)*

Even in Adam's day, millions of Saints—*all* of Adam's righteous posterity—attended this great spiritual meeting.[4] We can only imagine what this wonderful experience would have been like: gathering together with the rest of Adam's righteous posterity, hearing prophesies, seeing visions of the future, and hearing from and seeing Jesus Christ for ourselves.

> *"Adam-ondi-Ahman, of eternal fame, first comes to our at-*
> *tention because of a great conference held there by Father*
> *Adam in his day. Nearly a thousand years had then passed*
> *since the first man and the first woman had stepped from*
> *Eden's garden. We do not know how many million mortals*
> *made this earth their home in that day . . . we can suppose*
> *the population of the earth far exceeded that of later ages*
> *when the ills of the flesh set a limit on the numbers of men.*
> *And it is not unreasonable to suppose that the numbers of*
> *the righteous were exceedingly great.*
>
> *"We may not be amiss in supposing that many millions re-*
> *sponded to the call to come to a general conference in*
> *Adam-ondi-Ahman. This we do know, 'The Lord appeared*
> *unto them' – Jesus Christ their King stood in their midst.*
> *When the full account comes to us, we shall read of the testi-*
> *monies borne by both men and women; of great doctrinal ser-*
> *mons delivered; and of the outpouring of spiritual gifts upon*
> *the faithful then assembled. What visions they must have*
> *seen; what revelations they must have received; what feelings*
> *of rapture must have filled their bosoms as they feasted upon*
> *the things of eternity! All that happened at Adam-ondi-Ah-*
> *man in those early days was but a type and a shadow – a si-*
> *militude, if you will – of what shall happen at the same*
> *blessed place in the last days when Adam and Christ and the*

---

[4] See Note 2

residue of men who are righteous assemble again in solemn worship." (Millennial Messiah, p. 579)

Although this will be a "secret" meeting, as far as the world in general is concerned, *all faithful members of the Church will know about it and will take part in it.* This is new doctrine to some—that all faithful members of the Church will be invited to and participate in the General Conference that will officially place Jesus Christ at the head of the Kingdom of God on earth. There are many reasons for the necessity of this meeting, and for the requirement that *all* faithful members participate in this momentous meeting. The Lord has required the Church to follow certain procedures and formalities in order to make sure the Church organization is open and above reproach. One of those requirements is that any change in the leadership of the Church must be done openly and those in authority must be publicly sustained by the general membership of the Church.

> "Before the Lord Jesus descends openly and publicly in the clouds of glory, attended by all the hosts of heaven; before he stands on Mount Zion, or sets his feet on Olivet, before all flesh shall see him together; before any of his appearances, there is to be a secret appearance to selected members of his Church. He will come in private to his Prophet and the Apostles then living. Those who have held keys and powers and authorities in all ages from Adam to the represent will also be present. And further, all the faithful members of the Church then living and all the faithful saints of all the ages past will be present. It will be the greatest congregation of faithful saints ever assembled on planet earth. It will be a sacrament meeting. It will be a day of Judgment for the faithful of all the ages. And it will take place in Davies County, Missouri, at a place called Adam-ondi-Ahman." (Millennial Messiah, p. 578)

As noted in previous quotes, the Saints will not only have the opportunity to witness this great event, but will actively participate in it. All who hold the Priesthood will have the opportunity to sustain their new Priesthood Leader: Jesus Christ. In addition, all faithful members will participate in sustaining the new head of the Church: their King,

Jesus Christ. These acts of participation by faithful members of the church will be necessary in order to establish the legal and lawful position of Jesus Christ as head of the Kingdom of God on earth *prior* to His coming in glory.

> *"First of all let me say that this church organization I have described, while ordained of God, cannot subsist without the consent of the people. When the young Prophet Joseph contemplated the great work of organizing the church of Christ, he received a commandment from the Lord to the effect that he must call his brethren together who had received the gospel, and obtain their sanction to such a proceeding."* (B.H. Roberts, New Witnesses for God, 1:348)

> *"The eternal laws by which he and all others exist in the eternities of the Gods decree that the consent of the creature must be obtained before the Creator can rule perfectly."* (Brigham Young, Journal of Discourses, 15:134)

There will be many sessions in this meeting, and it will probably take many days, even months, to complete. Several of the sessions of this great Conference will be priesthood meetings, where faithful priesthood holders of all ages will make an accounting of their stewardships to their priesthood leaders—from the lowliest of elders up to the most honored Prophets of past dispensations.

> *"All who have held the keys of priesthood will then have to give an account to those from whom they received them. They will unite together in a general council to give an account of their stewardships, and as in the various ages men have received their power to administer from those who had previously held the keys thereof, there will be a general account . . . hence the elders give an account to presidents, and those presidents and the seventies give an account to the twelve apostles; the twelve to the First Presidency; and they to Joseph, from whom they, and the twelve, received their priesthood. Joseph delivers his authority to Peter, who held the keys before him, and delivered them to him; and Peter to Moses and Elias, who endowed him with this authority on the Mount; and they to those from whom they received them.*

And thus the world's affairs will be regulated and put right, the restitution of all things be accomplished, and the kingdom of God be ushered in. The earth will be delivered from under the curse, resume its paradisiacal glory, and all things pertaining to its restoration be fulfilled." (John Taylor, The Gospel Kingdom, p. 216)

After Christ is officially sustained and set apart as our King, he will begin the process of setting up his earthly throne by establishing a new government that will incorporate all of the laws and principles of the U.S. Constitution. Then, one by one, all nations will bow to its rule.[5]

"At this council Christ will be received and acknowledged as the rightful ruler of the earth. Following this event every government in the world, including the United States, will have to become part of the government of God. Then righteous rule will be established. The earth will be cleansed; the wicked will be destroyed; and the reign of peace will be ushered in." (Doctrines of Salvation 3:13)

The "Millennium" officially starts when Jesus Christ is sustained as head of the Church, and begins to reign personally on earth.

During the period immediately after this grand council, assignments will be given to 1) expand the city of New Jerusalem to prepare for the resurrection of the Church of the Firstborn (the morning of the First Resurrection); 2) prepare the Saints to receive their King when he comes in glory, by calling the 144,000 who will prepare the Saints to receive their Calling and Elections; and 3) prepare for the final conflict and destruction of the wicked by gathering and preparing the Army of God.

THE 144,000 HIGH PRIESTS

Part of the preparation and training the Saints must go through prior to the coming of Christ in glory will entail the calling of 144,000

---

[5] See Note 3

high priests that will lead the Saints who are prepared into the Church of the Firstborn.[6] These high priests will be called to teach the Saints how to make their Calling and Election sure. Then, the Saints will enter the temples of God and receive the "more sure word of prophesy:" they will be sealed to Eternal Life, they will officially become members of the Church of the Firstborn.

The "144,000" are high priests who have already made their Calling and Election sure. They serve in the temple, teaching the Saints of God how they, too, can obtain the assurance of eternal life. Then, they perform the priesthood ordinance that actually seals the Saints to eternal life.

> ". . . and there were sealed an hundred and forty and four thousand of all the tribes of the Children of Israel . . . these are they which came out of great tribulation, and have washed their robes, and made them white in the blood of the Lamb. Therefore are they before the throne of God, and serve him day and night in his temple: and he that sitteth on the throne shall dwell among them." (Revelation 7:1–16)

> "And I looked, and lo, a Lamb stood on the mount Zion, and with him an hundred forty and four thousand, having his Father's name written in their foreheads . . . ." (Revelation 14:1–5)

> "There will be 144,000 'saviors on Mount Zion,' and with them an innumerable host that no man can number. Oh, I beseech you to go forward, go forward and make your calling and your election sure." (DHC 6:365)

> "Q. What are we to understand by sealing the one hundred and forty-four thousand? A. We are to understand that those who are sealed are high priests, ordained unto the holy order of God, to administer the everlasting gospel . . . to whom is given power over the nations of the earth, to bring as many as will come to the Church of the Firstborn." (D&C 77:11)

---

[6] D&C 133:18

44

There have been and will be many millions of Saints who are sealed up to eternal life. It is from among these elect Saints that the Lord will choose 144,000 to teach others what they need to know to enter the "Church of the Firstborn," the highest degree in the Celestial Kingdom.

> "At this time Joseph Smith . . . indicated that the conferral of the fullness of the priesthood was a 'sealing . . . on top of the head,' of which the phrase 'sealed in their foreheads' was symbolic. Furthermore, Joseph Smith here taught that it was through the ordinance of conferral of the fullness of the priesthood that men could be qualified to be a part of the special missionary force of the last days which would number 144,000 high priests (D&C 77:8–11, 14) . . . on 4 February 1844, the Prophet indicated that 'the selection of the persons to form that number had already commenced.' He had already conferred these blessings on at least 17 men (History of the Church, 6:196 and Wilford Woodruff Journal, under date given)." (The Words of Joseph Smith, pg. 297)

> "Those who gain exaltation in the Celestial Kingdom are those who are members of the Church of the Firstborn. There will be many who are members of the Church of Jesus Christ of Latter-day Saints who shall never become members of the Church of the Firstborn. To become a member of the Church of the Firstborn is to become one of the inner circle.

> "The Lord has made it possible for all of us to become members of the Church of the Firstborn, by receiving the blessings of the house of the Lord and overcoming all things . . . they seal upon us the keys and powers which, through our obedience, entitle us to become sons and daughters and members of the Church of the Firstborn, receiving all things in the kingdom. This is what we can get in the Temple, so that we become members of the family, sons and daughters of God, not servants." (Doctrines of Salvation, 2:42)

We know the timetable of these events because we are told that the Lord will withhold the cataclysmic destructions prepared for the earth until *after* the saints are gathered to Zion and the 144,000 are sealed and have begun their work.

> *"And I saw another angel . . . saying, hurt not the earth, neither the sea, nor the trees, till we have sealed the servants of our God in their foreheads." (Revelation 7:3–4)*

It is during this time, while Jesus Christ remains upon the earth to direct the progress of his kingdom, that the saints enter the temples of God to purify themselves, gaining spiritual sustenance from the presence of the Lord and learning from the 144,000 high priests set apart to teach them. They obtain their Calling and Elections and are sealed up to eternal life by a priesthood ordinance.

It is also during this period of time that the Saints will build thousands of homes and buildings that will be inhabited and used by all the righteous people who will be resurrected when Christ comes in glory. In addition, many are set apart as soldiers in the Army of God, and are trained to perform a work of destruction when Christ and his army face the Anti-Christ in the final battle.

As the Saints continue their preparations and further build-up Zion (in America), on the other side of the world the Anti-Christ begins his march on Jerusalem. It is at this time that the Lord will set apart two of his servants, and send them to Israel to protect that nation from the evil descending upon them. These two servants or prophets are called to hold back the forces of evil until the Saints are prepared to go to war. (See *The Two Prophets,* p 65.)

After all the Saints are gathered and prepared, the Lord will finally release the destroying angels upon the inhabitants of the earth.

NATIONS UNITE TO WAR WITH ISRAEL

At the same time Christ is preparing his people in Zion, on the other side of the world the Anti-Christ is continuing to consolidate his power. Having seized control of most of the nations of the earth, he begins a campaign to destroy the nation of Israel. Remember, Israel is a powerful nation—with nuclear capability and the will to use it. The nations facing Israel know this, and know that before being destroyed, Israel will use all the weapons they possess to destroy their enemies.[7]

No nation will be neutral in this matter and all nations will side against Israel.

The army of the Anti-Christ will come from the north, the size of it so large (200 million) that it covers the land like a cloud.

> *"In that day when my people Israel dwelleth safely, thou shalt come from thy place out of the north parts, thou, and many people with thee. And thou shalt come up against my people of Israel, as a cloud to cover the land; it shall be in the latter days." (Ezekiel 38:15–16)*

> *"And the number of the army were two hundred thousand thousand: and I heard the number of them." (Revelation 9:16)*

As the Anti-Christ gathers his forces to come against Israel, Jesus Christ is dwelling in Zion, gathering and preparing his army of Saints. *Though living upon the earth, Christ has not as yet come "in Glory" to cleanse the earth.*

---

[7] Joel 3:1–2, 9

NOTES

1. Joseph Fielding Smith, *Church History and Modern Revelation,* Vol . 3:118.

    "There has been some confusion in the minds of many because the Prophet speaks of Tower Hill, and later after traveling some half mile and coming to Wight's Ferry, and marking off territory for a township he speaks of Spring Hill near said ferry. It has been thought that "Tower Hill" and "Spring Hill" are two separate places some half mile or so apart, but the place called by these two names is the same. Some hundred yards or more from the crest of the hill, was Lyman Wight's home, and on or near the top of the hill was the ruins of an ancient altar . . . at this place which the Prophet named Adam-ondi-Ahman. Adam-ondi-Ahman was not just a small spot resting on the brow of the hill, but this name has reference to the surrounding territory. One can obtain a beautiful view from this ancient altar overlooking the valley through which courses Grand River. It was in this valley where Adam called together the faithful of his posterity three years before his death and blessed them. (D& C 107:53) It will be in this same valley where the Ancient of Days shall sit at the grand gathering of the worthies who have held keys of the dispensations, and where Adam will make his report, likewise all others who have been given keys, and our Savior shall be crowned King of kings and take his place as the rightful ruler of the earth."

2. Bruce R. McConkie, *Promised Messiah,* pg. 607.

    "We do not know how many there were, and we do not say how many there were. But it is perfectly obvious there were 'many, exceeding great many.' (Alma 13:12) We do not know the population of the earth in the days before the flood. We do know that the childbearing years of women continued to great ages and that sufficient time was involved for great populations to arise. If the population of the earth had doubled every thirty-three years, from the day of Adam to the appearing of the Lord at Adam-ondi-Ahman, there would have been four and a half billion people on earth. We do not suppose for a moment that such was the case, but we cannot escape the conclusion that many people were then alive, and we do know that all the righteous among them saw the Lord."

3. Joseph Fielding Smith, *The Way to Perfection,* pp. 289–290.

    The Keys of The Everlasting Kingdom

    "In this council Christ will take over the reigns of government, officially, on this earth, and 'the kingdom and dominion, and the greatness of the kingdom under the whole heaven, shall be given to the people of the saints of the Most High, whose kingdom is an everlasting kingdom, and all dominions shall serve and obey him,' even Jesus Christ.

Thrones To Be Cast Down

"Until this grand council is held, Satan shall hold rule in the nations of the earth; but at that time thrones are to be cast down and man's rule shall come to an end—for it is decreed that the Lord shall make an end of all nations. (D&C 87:6) Preparation for this work is now going on. Kingdoms are already tottering, some have fallen; but eventually they shall all go the way of the earth, and he shall come whose right it is to rule. Then shall he give the government to the saints of the Most High.

By Voice of The Priesthood

"This council in the valley of Adam-ondi-Ahman is to be of the greatest importance to this world. At that time there will be a transfer of authority from the usurper and impostor, Lucifer, to the rightful King, Jesus Christ. Judgment will be set and all who have held keys will make their reports and deliver their stewardships, as they shall be required. Adam will direct this judgment, and then he will make his report, as the one holding the keys for this earth, to his Superior Officer, Jesus Christ. Our Lord will then assume the reins of government; directions will be given to the Priesthood; and He, whose right it is to rule, will be installed officially by the voice of the Priesthood there assembled."

Chapter Four
The Testimony of Disasters

After the Saints are told to gather to Zion and the missionaries are called home; and *after* Christ takes control of his Kingdom on earth (but before he comes in glory), there will be a period of time when the Lord will voice his own testimony by a series of destructive forces and plagues to be unleashed upon the earth.[1]

> "Then, when the saints have done all that in their power lies, both to preach the everlasting word and to build up the eternal kingdom; when they of themselves can no longer go forward with the decreed success attending their labors; when the wars and desolations and carnality of men are about to overwhelm them — then the Lord will take over. By his own power he will destroy the wicked, complete his strange act, and pour out the consumption decreed." (Millennial Messiah, p. 143)

> "It will be a sorry day for any nation, where the gospel is being preached, should it conclude to drive the elders of the Church from its borders and deny them the right to preach the gospel among the people. The elders insure peace unto the nations, so long as they will hear the message of salvation and will protect and defend the truth. When the time comes

---

[1] D&C 88:89, 92

51

that the nations will cast the elders out and no longer receive their testimony, but 'bow to Satan's thrall,' woe be unto them. We read in the word of the Lord that after the testimony of the elders will come wrath and indignation upon the people. For after their testimony will come the testimony of earthquakes, of thunderings, of lightnings, of tempests, of the waves of the sea heaving beyond their bounds. These things shall follow the testimony of the elders of the Church of Jesus Christ of Latter-day Saints, when the people of the world reject them and drive them from their borders." (Doctrines of Salvation 3:7)

We must assume that some of the righteous will be caught up in these events and some will even be killed. But we have received many promises that *most of the faithful saints will be spared.* Just as they were spared when the land of Zion was cleansed (during the Civil War), they will be spared because they followed the counsel of the Prophet and gathered to Zion. They will be spared because of their faith in Jesus Christ.[2]

"And the day shall come that the earth shall rest, but before that day the heavens shall be darkened, and a veil of darkness shall cover the earth; and the heavens shall shake, and also the earth; and great tribulations shall be among the children of men, but my people will I preserve." (Moses 7:61)

THE HALF HOUR OF SILENCE

Each of the judgments that will come upon men will be preceded by an angel sounding a trump of warning. The first trump will cause a period of silence for one half hour.

"And when he had opened the seventh seal, there was silence in heaven about the space of half an hour." (Revelation 8:1)

"What is meant by the half hour of silence has not yet been revealed. If it is to be reckoned on the basis of 'the Lord's

---

[2] 1 Nephi 22;19; see Note 1

> *time' of 1000 years to a day, the duration would be some 21 of our years."* (Doctrinal New Testament Commentary 3:499)

This period of silence seems to be caused by the wickedness that has come upon the earth. Perhaps it is the moment in time that the Anti-Christ consolidates his power and the nations of the earth decide to destroy Israel. Or perhaps it is the moment when the wheat and the tares have been separated (the wicked and righteous have gathered, one to the Anti-Christ and the other to Zion). The sound of the trumpet and the silence that follows, pierces each heart and makes men realize the paths they have chosen.

> *"For all flesh is corrupted before me; and the powers of darkness prevail upon the earth, among the children of men, in the presence of all the hosts of heaven--which causeth silence to reign, and all eternity is pained, and the angels are waiting the great command to reap down the earth, to gather the tares that they may be burned; and, behold, the enemy is combined."* (D&C 38:12)

> *"For I am no respecter of persons, and will that all men shall know that the day speedily cometh; the hour is not yet, but is nigh at hand, when peace shall be taken from the earth, and the devil shall have power over his own dominion. And also the Lord shall have power over his saints, and shall reign in their midst, and shall come down in judgment upon Idumea, or the world."* (D&C 1:35–36)

After the period of silence, a series of seven trumpets will sound, denoting seven desolations to come upon the earth. These periods of destruction are God's testimony of His power, and the reality of His existence. They are also part of the process that God will use to literally change the face of the earth, to make the earth like the garden of Eden.

> *"And I saw the seven angels which stood before God; and to them were given seven trumpets."* (Revelation 7:2)

These desolations will be accompanied by seven plagues, which are probably a direct result of the seven desolations.

> *"And I heard a great voice out of the temple saying to the seven angels, Go your ways, and pour out the vials of the wrath of God upon the earth." (Revelation 16:1)*

The exact timing of these disasters and plagues is not known, nor do we know all of the "natural" causes of these events. We know that the judgments will start *after* Christ comes to Adam-ondi-ahman, and will be part of His personal testimony to the world of the truthfulness of the Gospel. It is obvious that these desolations and plagues are linked together: *they are grouped into three great "Woes"* that cover long periods of time.

THE FIRST WOE

The first five trumpets that sound are called the *First Woe*. This is because all of the disasters symbolized by the first five trumpets are caused by one event: a *star* falling to the earth. This *star* seems to be a comet of considerable size, that may come as part of a larger meteor storm. What is clear is that this *heavenly body* will strike the earth with such force that the earth will actually be moved out of its natural orbit around the sun.

The effect of this comet upon the earth will begin before it actually hits the earth. As the tail of the *comet* approaches the earth (a comet's tail always points away from the sun), the material in the tail and its added gravitational pull will cause weather around the world to change, will cause earthquakes as the earth's plates move against each other, and will cause volcanoes to come violently back to life. This will result in great pollutions of both the air and the sea. And all of this will occur *prior* to the actual impact upon the earth.

> *"The first angel sounded, and there followed hail and fire mingled with blood, and they were cast upon the earth: and the third part of trees was burnt up, and all green grass was*

burnt up. And the second angel sounded, and as it were a great mountain burning with fire was cast into the sea; and the third part of the sea became blood." (Revelation 8:7–9)

"And there shall be a great hailstorm sent forth to destroy the crops of the earth." (D&C 29:16)

A description of the effects of a comet coming close to hitting the earth in ancient times is provided by Immanuel Velikovsky:

"In the middle of the second millennium before the present era, the earth underwent one of the greatest catastrophes in its history. A celestial body that only shortly before had become a member of the solar system — a new comet — came very close to the earth. The comet was on its way from its perihelion and touched the earth first with its gaseous tail. One of the first visible signs of this encounter was the reddening of the earth's surface by a fine dust of rusty pigment. In sea, lake, and river this pigment gave a bloody coloring to the water. Because of these particles . . . the world turned red.

"The presence of the hematoid pigment in the rivers caused the death of fish followed by decomposition and smell . . . The skin of men and of animals was irritated by the dust, which caused boils, sickness, and the death of cattle.

"Following the red dust, a 'small dust,' like 'ashes of the furnace,' fell 'in all the land of Egypt (Exodus 9:8),' and then a shower of meteorites flew toward the earth. Our planet entered deeper into the tail of the comet. The dust was a forerunner of the gravel. There fell 'a grievous hail, such as not been in Egypt since its foundations (Exodus 9:18)' . . . We are also informed by Midrashic and Talmudic sources that the stones which fell on Egypt were hot; this fits only meteorites, not a hail of ice. In the Scriptures it is said that these stones fell 'mingled with fire (Exodus 9:24),' and that their fall was accompanied by 'loud noises,' rendered as 'thunderings' . . . The fall of meteorites is accompanied by crashes or explosion-like noises, and in this case they were so 'mighty,' according to the Scriptural narrative, the people in

*the palace were terrified as much by the din of the falling
stones as by the destruction they caused (Exodus 9:28).*

*"A torrent of large stones coming from the sky, an earth-
quake, a whirlwind, a disturbance in the movement of the
earth — these four phenomena belong together. It appears that
a large comet must have passed very near to our planet and
disrupted its movement; a part of the stones dispersed in the
neck and tail of the comet smote the surface of our earth a
shattering blow.*

*"If the head of a comet should pass very close to our path, so
as to effect a distortion in the career of the earth, another phe-
nomenon besides the disturbed movement of the planet
would probably occur: a rain of meteorites would strike the
earth and would increase to a torrent. Stones scorched by
flying through the atmosphere would be hurled on home and
head. In the Book of Joshua, two verses before the passage
about the sun that was suspended on high for a number of
hours without moving to the Occident, we find this passage:
'As they (the Canaanite Kings) fled from before Israel, and
were in the going down to Beth-horon . . . the Lord cast down
great stones from heaven upon them unto Azekah, and they
died: they were more which died with hail stones than they
whom the children of Israel slew with the sword' (Joshua
10:11). The meteorites fell on the earth in a torrent. They
must have fallen in very great numbers for they struck down
more warriors than the swords of the adversaries. To have
killed persons by the hundreds or thousands in the field, a
cataract of stones must have fallen. Such a torrent of great
stones would mean that a train of meteorites or a comet had
struck our planet." (Worlds in Collision, pp 41–48, 51–53)*

The scriptures make it clear that the earth will "fall," or be moved
out of its present orbit. This change in the position of the earth will
reverse the effect that the fall of Adam and Eve had upon the earth
when Adam and Eve fell from grace in the garden of Eden. When
Adam and Eve sinned and were cast out of God's presence, the earth
itself was also cast out of God's presence: it was moved from an area
around Kolob, and sent to its current location in this solar system.

> *"This earth is our home, it was framed for the habitation of those who are faithful to God, and who prove themselves worthy to inherit the earth when the Lord shall have sanctified, purified and glorified it and brought it back into his presence, from which it fell far into space . . . When the earth was framed and brought into existence and man was placed upon it, it was near the throne of our Father in heaven. And when man fell . . . the earth fell into space, and took up its abode in this planetary system, and the sun became our light. This is the glory the earth came from, and when it is glorified it will return again unto the presence of the Father, and it will dwell there, and these intelligent beings that I am looking at, if they are worthy of it, will dwell upon this earth."*
> (Brigham Young, Journal of Discourses, 17:144)

Some time prior to the final judgment, the earth must make the journey back to Kolob. It is possible that when this star or comet hits the earth, it will be the natural cause that brings this event about. This is one possible scenario: the star will strike with such force that it will cause the earth to reel to and fro, and will move the earth out of its orbit around the sun. As tidal waves destroy the coastal cities of the continents, the earth will fall towards the sun, scorching the earth with heat. The earth will not hit the sun, but will pick up tremendous speed, and, with the added force of the sun's gravity, will—like a slingshot—be propelled away from the sun and towards the center of the Universe. As the earth moves away from the sun, the sun will grow darker and both the sun and the moon will turn blood red. (One of the unique properties of light, is that when an object is moving toward a light source, the light looks blue. If an object is moving away from the light, it looks red. Therefore, when the earth begins moving away from the sun, its light will look red.)[3]

> *"And the third angel sounded, and there fell a great star from heaven, burning as it were a lamp, and it fell upon the third part of the rivers, and upon the fountains of waters; and the name of the star was WORMWOOD: and the third part of he waters became wormwood (wormwood is a bitter*

---

[3] D&C 88:87

herb that made water undrinkable); and many men died of the waters, because they were made bitter. And the fourth angel sounded, and the third part of the sun was smitten, and the third part of the moon, and the third part of the stars; so as the third part of them was darkened, and the day shone not for a third part of it, and the night likewise." (Revelation 8:10–11)

"The earth shall reel to and fro like a drunkard, and shall be removed like a cottage; and the transgression thereof shall be heavy upon it; and it shall fall, and not rise again." (Isaiah 24:20)

"What becomes of the earth then? If the earth falls, which way will it go? Will not the greatest and most powerful planet attract it? . . . for the greater bodies attract the lesser. If the earth falls, and is not to rise again, it will be removed out of its present orbit. Where will it go? God says he will gather all things in one; then He will gather the earth likewise. The gathering will be upon a larger scale in time to come; for by and by the stars of Heaven will fall. Which way will they go? They will rally to a grand center, and there will be one grand constellation of worlds. What is He going to do with it? Why, take it where the sun will shine upon it continually, and there shall be no more night there; and the hand of God will wipe away the tears from all faces. Now, we have but one sun to shine upon us, but when the earth is taken out of this orbit, it will come in contact with the rays of other suns that illuminate other spheres; their rays will dazzle our earth, and make the glory of God rest upon it, so that there will be no more night there." (Orson Hyde, Journal of Discourses, 1:129)

The enormity of the events that will take place on the earth as a result of being hit by a star can hardly be fathomed. The actual movement of the earth will be affected, and thus the entire world will, in turn, be affected. Destruction on a scale unknown since the great flood will be experienced. Once again we turn to Velikovsky for a description:

"The problem before us is one of mechanics. Points on the outer layers of the rotating globe (especially near the equator) move at a higher linear velocity than points on the inner layers, but at the same angular velocity. Consequently, if the earth were suddenly stopped (or slowed down) in its rotation, the inner layers might come to rest (or their rotational velocity might be slowed) while the outer layers would still tend to go on rotating. This would cause friction between the various liquid or semifluid layers, creating heat; on the outermost periphery the solid layers would be torn apart, causing mountains and even continents to fall or rise . . . mountains fell and others rose from level ground; the earth with its oceans and continents became heated; the sea boiled in many places, and rock liquefied; volcanoes ignited and forests burned.

"Since the world survived, there must have been a mechanism to cushion the slowing down of terrestrial motion . . . or, if rotation persisted undisturbed, the terrestrial axis may have tilted in the presence of a strong magnetic field, so that the sun appeared to lose for hours its diurnal movement.

"The swift shifting of the atmosphere under the impact of the . . . comet, and the rush of the atmosphere resulting from inertia when the earth stopped rotating or shifted its poles, all contributed to produce hurricanes of enormous velocity and force and of worldwide dimensions.

"Manuscript Troano and other documents of the Mayas describe a cosmic catastrophe during which the ocean fell on the continent, and a terrible hurricane swept the earth. The hurricane broke up and carried away all towns and all forests. Exploding volcanoes, tides sweeping over mountains, and impetuous winds threatened to annihilate humankind . . . The face of the earth changed, mountains collapsed, other mountains grew and rose over the onrushing cataract of water driven from oceanic spaces, and a wild tornado moved through the debris descending from the sky.

"The ocean tides are produced by the action of the sun and to a larger extent by that of the moon. A body larger than the

moon or one nearer to the earth would act with greater effect. A comet with a head as large as the earth, passing suffi- ciently close, would raise the waters of the oceans miles high. The slowing down or stasis of the earth in its rotation would cause a tidal recession of water towards the poles, but the celestial body nearby would disturb this poleward recession, drawing the water toward itself.

"The Chinese annals say that in the time of Emperor Yahou the sun did not go down for ten days. The world was in flames, and 'in their vast extent' the waters 'overtopped the great heights, threatening the heavens with their floods.' The water of the ocean was heaped up and cast upon the conti- nent of Asia; a great tidal wave swept over the mountains and broke in the middle of the Chinese Empire. The water was caught in the valleys between the mountains, and the land was flooded for decades." (Worlds in Collision, *pp. 44, 67, 70–71)*

After the star hits the earth, and as a direct result of the earth- quakes and massive pollution from volcanoes, one-third of all green vegetation is destroyed, all of the earth's crops are destroyed, one-third of all of the life in the oceans is dead, one-third of all ocean vessels are destroyed, one-third of all water becomes undrinkable, and darkness covers the earth.

Then, as an *indirect* result of the star falling to earth, three plagues are created, causing further death and destruction.

"And the first went and poured out his vial upon the earth, and there fell an evil and grievous sore upon the men which had the mark of the beast, and upon them which worshiped his image. And the second angel poured out his vial upon the sea; and it became as the blood of a dead man: and every liv- ing soul died in the sea. And the third angel poured out his vial upon the rivers and fountains of waters; and they be- came blood." (Revelation 16:2)

In speculating on how the Earth will make its way back to Kolob, and the "natural" process by which these events will take place, we might assume that after the earth is moved out of its orbit, it will naturally be attracted to the largest gravity source in the area—the sun. As it draws near to the sun, men are burned with heat and the weather on the earth changes again. For at least one year there is no rain upon the earth and the covenant of the "rainbow" will disappear. As the earth moves around the far side of the sun, the gravitational pull will serve to produce a "slingshot" effect that hurls the earth at tremendous speed towards the center of the universe, back to Kolob.

> "And the fourth angel poured out his vial upon the sun; and power was given unto him to scorch men with fire. And men were scorched with great heat, and blasphemed the name of God, which hath power over these plagues: and they repented not." (Revelation 16:8)

> "I have asked the Lord concerning His coming . . . and while asking the Lord, He gave a sign and said, '. . . in any year that the bow should be seen the Lord would not come; but whenever you see the bow withdrawn, it shall be a token that there shall be famine, pestilence, and great distress among the nations, and that the coming of the Messiah is not far distant.'" (The Prophet Joseph Smith, p. 340)

As the earth recovers from the impact of the comet, darkness veils the earth and Satan's power is unleashed in all its fury. God does not stay his hand; a plague of insects is cast upon the earth, perhaps brought by the comet itself.

> "And the fifth angel sounded, and I saw a star fall from heaven unto the earth: and to him was given the key to the bottomless pit. And he opened the bottomless pit; and there arose a smoke out of the pit . . . and there came out of the smoke locusts upon the earth: and unto them was given power, as the scorpions of the earth have power. And it was commanded them that they should not hurt the earth, but only those men which have not the seal of God in their foreheads. And in those days shall men seek death, and shall not find it; and shall desire to die, and death shall flee from them. And they had a king over them, which is the angel of the

bottomless pit, whose name is Abaddon (Satan)." (Revelation 9:1–11)

"The question arises here whether or not the comet . . . infested the earth with vermin which it may have carried in its trailing atmosphere in the form of larvae together with stones and gases . . . The persistence with which the (comet) is associated with a fly in the traditions of the peoples of both hemispheres . . . create the impression that the flies in the tail of (the comet) were not merely the earthly brood, swarming in heat like other vermin, but guests from another planet." (Worlds in Collision, pp. 185–186)

"And the fifth angel poured out his vial upon the seat of the beast; and his kingdom was full of darkness; and they gnawed their tongues for pain, and blasphemed the God of heaven because of their pains and their sores, and repented not of their deeds." (Revelation 16:10)

The aftermath of the destruction caused by the comet will continue to effect the earth for a long time. The first woe is over, but there are two more woes to come.

"One woe is past; and behold, there come two woes more hereafter." (Revelation 9:12)

THE SECOND WOE

The second Woe is a series of wars that cause destruction and additional plagues to come upon the earth. This woe begins with the rise of the Anti-Christ and culminates in the siege of Jerusalem and in the long awaited clash between Jesus Christ and the Anti-Christ: *the Battle of Armageddon.* This woe includes all of the wars that brought the Anti-Christ to power, up to and including the last great battle that will bring an end to his power. These wars will undoubtedly include the use of nuclear and chemical weapons (the descriptions of fire and pillars of smoke would accurately describe the effects of a nuclear bomb), and will eventually cause the death of one-third of all people living at the time. An indirect result of the wars and the millions of dead and decaying bodies left to rot upon the ground is a new series of plagues that ravage the earth, causing almost indescribable suffering and even more death. This period of warfare covers a long period of time. Many of the plagues will occur during the war, just as many of the events that have already been described as part of the first "Woe" will be happening concurrently.

> *"And the sixth angel sounded . . . loose the four angels which are bound in the bottomless pit. And four angels were loosed, for to slay the third part of men. And the number of the army of the horsemen were two hundred thousand thousand...and by these three was the third part of men killed: by the fire, and by the smoke, and by the brimstone. And the rest of the men which were not killed by these plagues yet repented not of the works of their hands . . . Neither repented they of their murders, nor of their sorceries, nor of their fornication, nor of their thefts." (Revelation JST 9:13–21)*

> *"And I will show wonders in the heavens and in the earth, blood, and fire, and pillars of smoke. The sun shall be turned into darkness, and the moon into blood, before the great and the terrible day of the Lord come." (Joel 2:30–31)*

The wars will have been raging for years, from the time the Anti-Christ and his three prophets consolidated their power by convincing the ten coalition nations to join them, through the years of persecuting the Saints and Jews, until they finally complete their work of destruction by marching on Jerusalem. As one of their final acts of world domination, the Anti-Christ will turn his sights on the nation of Israel. With an army of some 200 million, the Anti-Christ will come down from the north, destroying everything that tries to resist his progress. The blood and carnage will be beyond description, and it will end—briefly—at the siege of Jerusalem.[4]

> *"Behold, I will make Jerusalem a cup of trembling unto all the people round about, when they shall be in the siege both*

---

[4] Ezekiel 38:1–2, 15, 21

> *against Judah and against Jerusalem. And in that day will I
> make Jerusalem a burdensome stone for all people: all that
> burden themselves with it shall be cut in pieces, though all
> the people of the earth be gathered together against
> it." (Zechariah 12:2–3)*

When the Anti-Christ nears Jerusalem, the two "servants" that
were sent by Christ to protect Jerusalem prevent the advance of the
army. This becomes a two-edged sword, for while these two Prophets
use their power to delay the utter destruction of the Jews, their work
creates a state of siege in the city. This siege will last 3½ years. The
conditions inside the city during the siege become so terrible that
those left alive in the city turn to cannibalism to stay alive. All of these
events were prophesied and described in detail by Moses and others.[5]

> *". . . and the holy city shall they tread under foot forty and
> two months (3½ years)." (Revelation 11:2)*

> *"The Lord shall bring a nation against thee from far, from
> the end of the earth, as swift as the eagle flieth; a nation
> whose tongue thou shalt not understand; a nation of fierce
> countenance, which shall not regard the person of the old,
> nor shew favour to the young: and he shall eat the fruit of thy
> cattle, and the fruit of thy land, until thou be destroyed. And
> he shall besiege thee in all thy gates, until thy high and
> fenced walls come down, wherein thou trustedst, throughout
> all thy land: and he shall besiege thee in all thy gates
> throughout all thy land, which the Lord thy God hath given
> thee. And thou shalt eat the fruit of thine own body, the flesh
> of thy sons and of thy daughters, which the Lord thy God
> hath given thee, in the siege, and in the straitness, wherewith
> thine enemies shall distress thee: so that the man that is ten-
> der among you, and very delicate, his eye shall be evil toward
> his brother . . . so that he will not give to any of them of the
> flesh of his children whom he shall eat: because he hath noth-
> ing left him in the siege, wherewith thine enemies shall dis-
> tress thee in all thy gates. The tender and delicate woman
> among you, which would not adventure to set the sole of her*

---

[5] Zechariah 14:2–3

> foot upon the ground for delicateness and tenderness, her eye
> shall be evil toward the husband of her bosom, and toward
> her son, and toward her daughter, and toward her young one
> that cometh out from between her feet, and toward her chil-
> dren which she shall bear: for she shall eat them for want of
> all things secretly in the siege, wherewith thine enemy shall
> distress thee in thy gates." (Deuteronomy 28:49–53)

During this long war millions of people will die. The swiftness
with which the armies move in their quest for power, and the sheer
numbers of the dead both from the war and the natural calamities
happening around the world, leave no choice but to let the dead bodies decay as they lay on the ground. These bodies will end up creating
a plague of flies that begin to destroy the wicked as they continue to
seek the destruction of the Jews. In addition, we find what could only
be vivid descriptions of the effects of the nuclear and chemical weapons being used.

> "And it shall come to pass, because of the wickedness of the
> world, that I will take vengeance upon the wicked, for they
> will not repent; for the cup of mine indignation is full; for
> behold, my blood shall not cleanse them if they hear me not.
> Wherefore, I the Lord God will send forth flies upon the face
> of the earth, which shall take hold of the inhabitants thereof,
> and shall eat their flesh, and shall cause maggots to come in
> upon them; and their tongues shall be stayed that they shall
> not utter against me; and their flesh shall fall from off their
> bones, and their eyes from their sockets; and it shall come to
> pass that the beasts of the forest and the fowls of the air shall
> devour them up. And the great and abominable church,
> which is the whore of all the earth, shall be cast down by de-
> vouring fire, for abominations shall not reign." (D&C
> 29:17–21)

The Two Prophets

After Christ came secretly to Zion (America) and received the keys
of authority at Adam-ondi-Ahman, he set apart two "servants" and

sent them to protect Israel. It is during the 3½ years of the siege that they save the Jews from utter destruction. The scriptures make clear that these "two sons" or prophets are not Jews. They come from afar, and are sent to preach the gospel as well as protect the nation of Israel. It seems logical that these "prophets" would be members of The Church of Jesus Christ of Latter-day Saints—men in authority, called as prophets, seers, and revelators: in other words, Apostles of the Lord Jesus Christ.[7]

> "What is to be understood by the two witnesses, in the eleventh chapter of revelation? They are two prophets that are to be raised up to the Jewish nation in the last days, at the time of the restoration, and to prophesy to the Jews after they are gathered and have built the city of Jerusalem in the land of their fathers." (D&C 77:15)

> "Who will these witnesses be? We do not know, except that they will be followers of Joseph Smith; they will hold the holy Melchizedek Priesthood; they will be members of the Church of Jesus Christ of Latter-day Saints. It is reasonable to suppose, knowing how the Lord has always dealt with his people in all ages, that they will be two members of the Council of the Twelve or of the First Presidency of the Church."
> (Millennial Messiah, p. 390)

As holders of the Melchizedek Priesthood, the two Prophets have been given the authority to protect the city through the use of miraculous powers.

> "And I will give power unto my two witnesses, and they shall prophesy, clothed in sackcloth. And if any man will hurt them, fire proceedeth out of their mouth, and devoureth their enemies. These have power to shut heaven, that it rain not in the days of their prophecy: and have power over waters to turn them to blood, and to smite the earth with all plagues, as often as they will." (Revelation 11:3)

---

[7] Zechariah 13:7–9; 2 Nephi 8:17–20

Finally, the hand of the Lord is withdrawn, and the city is left without hope. The army of the Anti-Christ is permitted to kill the two Prophets, plunder the city, and desecrate the newly rebuilt temple of the Lord. This is the time of Satan's greatest power on earth. The Anti-Christ controls all the earth (with the exception of the land of Zion), has destroyed all but a few of the Jews, and occupies the Temple of God, using it as his personal throne. There is only one place of power left on earth for the Anti-Christ to overcome: Zion and Jesus Christ himself.

It is at this period of time that the Lord will come in glory, with Michael and an army of angels, *to the City of New Jerusalem.* The morning of the First Resurrection will begin, and the two prophets (who have been left lying dead in the street for three days) are resurrected in full view of those that killed them. This great climax at both ends of the earth will occur almost at the same time: Satan rules through his Anti-Christ, setting up his throne in the Temple at Jerusalem;[8] and Christ returns in glory with all the hosts of heaven to the faithful saints in Zion. Both Christ and the Anti-Christ then prepare for the final confrontation, to see who will rule the earth.[9]

> *"And when they shall have finished their testimony, the beast that ascendeth out of the bottomless pit shall make war against them, and shall overcome them, and kill them. And their dead bodies shall lie in the street of the great city, where also our Lord was crucified. And they of the people and kindreds and tongues and nations shall see their dead bodies three days and an half, and shall not suffer their dead bodies to be put in graves. And they that dwell upon the earth shall rejoice over them, and make merry, and shall send gifts one to another; because these two prophets tormented them that dwelt on the earth. And after three days and an half the spirit of life from God entered into them, and they stood upon their feet; and great fear fell upon them which saw them. And they heard a great voice from heaven saying unto them, Come up hither. And they ascended up to heaven in a cloud; and their*

---

[8] JST Matthew 1:32
[9] D&C 1:35

enemies beheld them. And the same hour was there a great earthquake, and the tenth part of the city fell." (Revelation 11:7)

"And I saw heaven opened, and behold a white horse; and he that sat upon him was called Faithful and True, and in righteousness he doth judge and make war. And he hath on his vesture and on his thigh a name written, King of Kings, and Lord of Lords. And I saw the beast, and the kings of the earth, and their armies, gathered together to make war against him that sat on the horse, and against his army." (Revelation 19:1–21)

"The second woe is past; and behold the third woe cometh quickly." (Revelation 11:14)

The Great Sign in Heaven

After the death of the two prophets in Israel, the Anti-Christ sets up his throne in the Temple of God in Jerusalem; the world rejoices and the power of darkness reigns over the earth. Then, a great sign appears in heaven that all the world will see. It will appear to the people of the earth as if another star or comet was falling to the earth, but it will be Jesus Christ. Remember—and picture in your mind—that Jesus Christ is a Man, about six feet tall; and even though he comes in glory, the people of the earth will not "see" him, but will only see his glory, or the light emanating from him.[10] Only the Saints, or those in tune with the Spirit of God, will know what and who it is that comes.[11]

"Immediately after the tribulation of those days shall the sun be darkened, and the moon shall not give her light, and the stars shall fall from heaven, and the powers of the heavens shall be shaken: and then shall appear the sign of the Son of man in heaven: and then shall all the tribes of the earth

---

[10] Revelation 1:7; D&C 29:11, 45:44
[11] D&C 88:92–93

mourn, and they shall see the Son of Man coming in the clouds of heaven with power and great glory." (Matthew 24:29-30)

*". . . then will appear one grand sign of the Son of Man in heaven. But what will the world do? They will say it is a planet, a comet, etc. But the Son of man will come as the sign of the coming of the Son of Man, which will be as the light of the morning cometh out of the east." (*The Prophet Joseph Smith, p. 287)

"When Jesus makes his next appearance upon the earth, but few of this Church will be prepared to receive him and see him face to face and converse with him; but he will come to his temple . . . Will the wicked know of it? They will know just as much about that as they now know about 'Mormonism,' and no more." (Brigham Young, Journal of Discourses, 7:142)

The One Half Hour of Silence

With the sounds of the trumpets of judgments in the air and the sign of the Son of Man being witnessed around the world, fear falls upon the wicked and in stunned silence the world waits to see what effect—what great disaster—will come upon them next.

"And another angel shall sound his trump, and all nations shall hear it. And there shall be silence in heaven for the space of half an hour; and immediately after shall the curtain of heaven be unfolded, as a scroll, and the face of the Lord shall be unveiled." (D&C 88:95)

THE THIRD WOE

The third Woe is Jesus Christ. He will come in glory at the climax of the siege at Jerusalem. He will bring with him all of the Saints that have already been resurrected (such as the Twelve Apostles and the

Twelve Disciples, and all of the righteous dead who were resurrected at the time of Christ's resurrection), and Michael (or Adam) and all of the hosts of angels assigned to this earth. In addition, Christ will also bring with him the City of Enoch, and the large land mass upon which it rests. This glorious entourage will descend with Christ and in glory. There is no doubt that the whole world will see this event. Because of the City of Enoch, it will look like a comet to people on the earth. After this great sign and the half hour period of silence, the veil of darkness is rent, the heavens unfold like a scroll, and the face of God is unveiled. Then Christ will descend with a shout *into the City of New Jerusalem.*[12]

Christ's presence and voice will cause the mountains to move, the continents to begin to come together again, and a shaking of the very earth itself—the largest earthquake ever known. There will be the sound of a trump—*the First Trump*—signaling the start of the First Resurrection. The righteous spirits in Paradise (part of the Spirit World) have also seen Jesus Christ coming. Their faith and love for the Savior will break the bonds that hold them, and they will reenter their bodies, burst from their graves, and rise to meet Christ in the air (the two prophets who lie dead in the streets of Jerusalem rise at this time also). Then those saints who remain alive on the earth, through their faith and love for their God, will also be caught up into the air to gather with them.

> *"And there shall be silence in heaven for the space of half an hour; and immediately after shall the curtain of heaven be unfolded, as a scroll is unfolded after it is rolled up, and the face of the Lord shall be unveiled; and the saints that are upon the earth, who are alive, shall be quickened and be caught up to meet him. And they who have slept in their graves shall come forth, for their graves shall be opened; and they also shall be caught up to meet him in the midst of the pillar of heaven — they are Christ's, the first fruits, they who shall descend with him first, and they who are on the earth*

---

[12] Revelation 6:14–16; D&C 38:8

*and in their graves, who are first caught up to meet him; and
all this by the voice of the sounding of the trump of the angel
of God." (D&C 88:95–96)*

*". . . it hath gone forth in a firm decree, that mine apostles,
the Twelve which were with me in my ministry at Jerusalem,
shall stand at my right hand at the day of my coming in a
pillar of fire." (D&C 29:12)*

*"And Enoch also, the seventh from Adam, prophesied of
these, saying, Behold, the Lord cometh with ten thousands of
his saints." (Jude 1:14)*

*"For the Lord himself shall descend from heaven with a
shout, with the voice of the archangel, and with the trump of
God: and the dead in Christ shall rise first: then they who are
alive, shall be caught up together into the clouds with them
who remain, to meet the Lord in the air; and so shall we be
ever with the Lord." (1 Thessalonians 4:16–17)*

*". . . all flesh shall see the glory of the Lord; when he reveals
himself the second time, every eye, not only those living at
that time in the flesh, in mortality on the earth, but also the
very dead themselves will also see him at that time." (Orson
Pratt,* Journal of Discourses, *18:170)*

The great earthquake that occurs at Christ's coming in glory af-
fects the entire world. It has a purpose: it prepares the earth to give up
the bodies of the righteous Saints in the first resurrection. Valleys are
raised, mountains are made low, and the continents of the earth begin
to come together into one land mass. This is another of the many steps
that will literally change the face of the earth, to make the earth like
the Garden of Eden.

*"And the seventh angel poured out his vial into the air; and
there came a great voice out of the temple of heaven, from the
throne, saying, It is done. And there were voices, and thun-
ders, and lightnings; and there was a great earthquake, such
as was not since men were upon the earth, so mighty an
earthquake and so great. And the great city was divided into*

three parts, and the cities of the nations fell; and every island fled away, and the mountains were not found." (Revelation 16:19)

"This is the time when earth's land masses shall unite; when islands and continents shall become one land; when every valley shall be exalted and every mountain shall be made low; when the rugged terrain of today shall level out into a millennial garden; when the great deep shall be driven back into its own place in the north. It is no wonder that the earthquake shall exceed all others in the entire history of the world." (Millennial Messiah, p. 397)

The City of Enoch Returns

The City of Enoch, and the land it rests upon, was translated (or taken up to heaven) prior to the great flood in the days of Noah. They were actually lifted off the earth and moved to another place. When this large city and land mass returns to the earth, it will return to the same place it left: the Gulf of Mexico. If you look at a map of the world, the western continents of North and South America fit like a puzzle into the eastern continents of Europe and Africa. When the Lord comes, the Atlantic Ocean will disappear as the two continents move back together. Just as it was in the days of Peleg, the earth will be one great land mass. There is, however, one large gap in the earth when all of the pieces are put together: the gulf of Mexico.

"And the Lord said unto Enoch: then shalt thou and all thy city meet them there, and we will receive them into our bosom, and they shall see us; and we will fall upon their necks, and they shall fall upon our necks, and we will kiss each other; and there shall be mine abode, and it shall be Zion, which shall come forth out of all the creations which I have made; and for the space of a thousand years the earth shall rest." (Moses 7:63–64)

After the Saints (both alive and dead) meet Christ and the City of Enoch in the pillar of heaven, they will descend to the City of Zion rejoicing. Tables will be prepared and a sacrament meeting will be held. The long awaited day has arrived, and all of the righteous Saints—both mortal and immortal—will rejoice for a thousand years.

> "And the graves of the saints shall be opened; and they shall come forth and stand on the right hand of the Lamb, when he shall stand upon Mount Zion, and upon the holy city, the New Jerusalem; and they shall sing the song of the Lamb, day and night forever and ever." (D&C 133:56)

> "After all nations have heard the proclamation (trumpet), there will be silence in the heavens. Then, the curtain of heaven will be unfolded as a scroll that is rolled up, and our Savior, our Redeemer, will unveil his face. He will appear as a being whose splendor and glory will cause the sun to hide his face with shame. Who will be with Jesus when he appears?. . . the Apostles who were with me in Jerusalem, all the former-day Saints, Enoch and his city, Abraham, Isaac, and Jacob. Latter-day Saints living upon the earth will ascend and mingle themselves with that vast throng; for they will be filled with anxiety to go where the Saints of the Church of the Firstborn are. About the same time, there will be Saints that have slumbered, and they are to be quickened and taken up into the heavens. The mortal Saints will then be transfigured and sanctified, but not immortalized. They will be prepared for the millennial reign. The tables will then be spread, and the Latter-day and Former-day Saints will be together to partake of the sacrament just as it is this afternoon." (Orson Pratt, Journal of Discourses, 8:51–52)

The First Resurrection

When Christ comes in glory, the First Resurrection will begin. This cannot be a haphazard or unorganized event. The Lord and the saints living on earth prior to his coming in glory have prepared for those who will be resurrected and live during the Millennium: homes will have to be provided; assignments and duties laid out for those who would be coming; arrangements made for families to find each other, etc. There are also children that will need to be cared for. When the resurrection occurs, the dead will be raised just as they were laid down—the body cannot grow or change in the grave. Therefore, all who have died as children will be resurrected as children, and they will have to be raised by loving parents until they physically grow into maturity. They will be taken care of by their own parents (if their parents are worthy to live during the Millennium), or by other righteous saints that will be assigned to take care of them.

> *"Bodies will come up, of course, as they were laid down, but will be restored to their proper, perfect frame immediately. Of course, children who die do not grow in the grave. They will come forth with their bodies as they were laid down, and then they will grow to the full stature of manhood or womanhood after the resurrection, but all will have their bodies fully restored."* (Doctrines of Salvation 2:292)

The First Resurrection will not happen all at once because there are just too many people that will be involved and it would be too confusing. We have already been told that there will be at least two resurrections: the resurrection of the Just and the resurrection of the Unjust. The righteous will be raised in a first "general" resurrection at the beginning of the Millennium, and the unrighteous will be raised in a second "general" resurrection at the end of the Millennium.

> *"And have hope toward God, that there shall be a resurrection of the dead, both of the Just and the Unjust."* (Acts 24:15)

Because of the preparation required, the First Resurrection will take place in several phases and will last almost the entire thousand years of Christ's reign upon the earth. Christ will resurrect the leadership of the Church first (those who have already earned a Celestial reward), so that they can be used to help organize those who will be resurrected later. This group of leaders are known as those who will come forth in "the morning of the first resurrection," and are those who belong to "the Church of the Firstborn." All who are resurrected at this time will be of a Celestial order.

All who are to be resurrected in a Celestial body must first have their temple endowments completed, either in person or by proxy. Those not so prepared at the time of Christ's coming will have to wait to be resurrected until their temple work is done. Then, as the Saints on earth complete the temple work for the living and the dead, they will be permitted to be raised from the dead. This is why temple work is so important: if it is not done now, people will have to wait to escape their spirit prison.

After the resurrection of those who belong to the Church of the Firstborn, and they in turn have completed all other preparations necessary, other phases of the First Resurrection will begin. These will include the rest of the Celestial order (those who will go to the Celestial kingdom, but not to the highest degree in that Kingdom; and those people who did not yet have their temple work done); those of a Terrestrial order, and the Heathen Nations (or those who never knew the commandments, or right from wrong). This general resurrection will proceed slowly, orderly, and will take hundreds of years to complete.

> "RESURRECTION OF CELESTIAL BODIES. At the time
> of the coming of Christ, they who shall descend with him
> first, are the just, 'whose names are written in heaven.' Following this great event, and after the Lord and the righteous
> who are caught up to meet him have descended upon the
> earth, there will come to pass another resurrection. In this
> resurrection will come forth those of the terrestrial order,
> who were not worthy to be caught up to meet him, but who
> are worthy to come forth to enjoy the millennial reign. This
> other class, are those who are not members of the 'Church of
> the Firstborn,' but who have led honorable lives."
> (Doctrines of Salvation 2:296)

Christ has come in glory, the "Church of the Firstborn" has been resurrected, and the Saints (both mortal and immortal) are organized and prepared. Those who will go with Christ to Jerusalem are selected, and the *Army of the Lord* prepares to march on Jerusalem to destroy the Anti-Christ and his army. The final battle is at hand.

NOTES

1. Joseph Fielding Smith, *Doctrines of Salvation*, Vol. 3:43.
    "WILL SAINTS ESCAPE LATTER-DAY PERILS? What about the Latter-day Saints? In one passage that I have read it says that the saints will hardly escape. Well, I do not think they are going to escape. I will tell you why: 'For the indignation of the Lord is kindled against their abominations and all their wicked works.' (That is the people of the earth.) 'Nevertheless, Zion shall escape if she observe to do all things whatsoever I have commanded her. But if she observe not to do whatsoever I have commanded her, I will visit her according to all her works, with sore affliction, with pestilence, with plague, with sword, with vengeance, with devouring fire. Nevertheless, let it be read this once to her ears, that I, the Lord, have accepted of her offering; and if she sin no more none of these things shall come upon her.' That was said over 120 years ago—in 1833. The Lord made the promise to the Latter-day Saints that if they would keep his commandments, they should escape when these destructions like a whirlwind should come suddenly--when all these trials and sufferings should come upon the people of the earth, the Latter-day Saints might escape if they would keep his commandments."

Bruce R. McConkie, *Doctrinal New Testament Commentary*, 3:503.
    "During this particular period of the war and desolation the evil forces will be directed against all men, *save those sealed up unto eternal life*, for those in Zion shall be preserved. The plagues and torments of this era shall so afflict men that they shall desire to die rather than to suffer more."

Chapter Five
The Arm of the Lord Falls Upon the Nations

After the Lord comes in glory and is received by his Saints, and *after* the First Resurrection begins, and *after* the face of the earth has been changed by the massive earthquake that accompanied his coming, the Lord and his army will begin to cleanse the earth of the wicked. Remember, the Anti-Christ still has great power and most of the people on the earth still follow him. Although aware of the supernatural events taking place at Christ's coming, most of the people still alive upon the earth do not understand the significance of those events. The coming of Jesus Christ and most of the other miraculous events that occurred at his coming took place in America—on the other side of the earth. The wicked would have seen the great sign in Heaven and seen Christ's glory when he came, but would not have recognized the event for what it really was. Although experiencing the earthquakes, plagues, and other destructions that were occurring daily—and even seeing the physical resurrection of some of the Saints—they will not understand, they will not change or repent; they will only fear.[1]

> "But before the arm of the Lord shall fall, an angel shall
> sound his trump, and the saints that have slept shall come
> forth to meet me in the cloud. Then shall the arm of the Lord

---

[1] D&C 29:9, 11–12, 21; 2 Thessalonians 1:7–8

> *fall upon the nations. And then shall the Lord set his foot upon this mount (the mount of Olives), and it shall cleave in twain, and the earth shall tremble, and reel to and fro, and the heavens also shall shake." (D&C 45:45–48)*

> *"Then shall the Lord go forth, and fight against those nations, as when he fought in the day of battle." (Zechariah 14:3)*

It will be a dramatic and vivid scene. The earth is moving away from the sun, and the world is in darkness. The earth is full of pollution and the ground is covered with dead and decaying bodies. But the City of Zion is a beacon of light in this darkness, and when Christ and his army leave for the final battle, the sheer force of their presence and spiritual power creates terror like rolling thunder before them. As Christ and his army march toward Jerusalem, they destroy everyone and everything in their path, cleansing and burning the earth as they go.[2] Because of the peculiar makeup of this army, mortals that have been transfigured (in the same way Enoch and his city were 'translated' or changed from a telestial state into a terrestrial state), as well as resurrected and Celestial beings who cannot be killed or hurt, this will be an army that cannot be defeated.[3]

> *"Blow ye the trumpet in Zion, and sound an alarm in my holy mountain; let all the inhabitants of the land tremble: for the day of the Lord cometh, for it is nigh at hand; a day of darkness and of gloominess, a day of clouds and of thick darkness, as the morning spread upon the mountains: a great people and strong; there hath not been ever the like, neither shall be any more after it, even to the years of many generations. A fire devoureth before them; and behind them a flame burneth: the land is as the garden of Eden before them, and behind them a desolate wilderness; yea, and nothing shall escape them. The appearance of them is as the appearance of horses; like the noise of chariots on the tops of mountains shall they leap, like the noise of a flame of fire that devoureth the stubble, as a strong people set in battle array. Before their*

---

[2] Psalm 50:3–5; see Note 1
[3] Isaiah 13:2–15

face the people shall be much pained; all faces shall gather blackness. They shall run like mighty men; they shall climb the wall like men of war; and they shall march every one on his ways, and they shall not break their ranks, and when they fall upon the sword, they shall not be wounded. The earth shall quake before them; the heavens shall tremble; the sun and the moon shall be dark, and the stars shall withdraw their shining; and the Lord shall utter his voice before his army; for his camp is very great; for he is strong that executeth his word; for the day of the Lord is great and very terrible; and who can abide it?"

". . . for the presence of the Lord shall be as the melting fire that burneth, and as the fire which causeth the waters to boil." (D&C 133:41)

"For behold, the Lord will come with fire, and with his chariots like a whirlwind, to render his anger with fury, and his rebuke with flames of fire. For by fire and by his sword will the Lord plead with all flesh; and the slain of the Lord shall be many." (Isaiah 66:15–16)

"And they shall go into the holes of the rocks, and into the caves of the earth, for fear of the Lord, and for the glory of his majesty, when he ariseth to shake terribly the earth." (Isaiah 2:19)

This scene of destruction and death is probably a new concept for some. Many have pictured the coming of Christ and the destruction of the wicked as being quick, neat, and bloodless. They believe that when Christ comes again, His glory and the sheer power of His presence would automatically "cleanse" the earth of all of the wicked. We were not to have anything to do with this great act of cleansing the earth. But this scenario is just not true. It reminds me of how people see and remember the "cleansing" of the wicked that occurred after Moses came down from Mount Sinai with the Ten Commandments. Because of the famous movie, everyone thinks the wicked were killed by a great earthquake; in other words, God killed the wicked and the righteous did not have to "dirty their hands" with this terrible act. But the truth is very different, both in Moses' time and in ours.

> *"And it came to pass, as soon as he came nigh unto the camp, that he saw the calf, and the dancing: and Moses' anger waxed hot, and he cast the tables out of his hands, and brake them beneath the mount . . . Then Moses stood in the gate of the camp, and said, Who is on the Lord's side? Let him come unto me. And all the sons of Levi gathered themselves together unto him. And he said unto them, Thus saith the Lord God of Israel, Put every man his sword by his side, and throughout the camp, and slay every man his brother, and every man his companion, and every man his neighbor. And the children of Levi did according to the word of Moses: and there fell of the people that day about three thousand men." (Exodus 32:19–29)*

Not only was it the righteous followers of God that carried out the destruction of the wicked in the days of Moses (and note that it was the Levites that were the most faithful, and were later rewarded by being the only ones to hold the Priesthood), but it will be the righteous Saints of our day that will go with Christ and literally carry out the destruction of the wicked by their own hands.[4]

The destruction of the wicked must of necessity be by the shedding of blood. This is due to the little understood doctrine of blood atonement. From the time of Adam there have been sins that could not be forgiven, sins that were so serious in nature that the Atonement of Christ could not provide a means of forgiveness for them. The only possible way that the spiritual effects of these sins could be reversed was through the shedding of their own blood. In order to cleanse the earth, and at the same time provide a possibility of redemption for the wicked that are killed, their blood must be shed.[5]

> *"And almost all things are by the law purged with blood; and without shedding of blood is no remission." (Hebrews 9:22)*

---

[4] Isaiah 34:2–5; Hebrews 9:22
[5] Genesis 9:6

"Are you aware that there are certain sins that man may commit for which the atoning blood of Christ does not avail? If then he would be saved he must make sacrifice of his own life to atone – so far as in his power lies – for that sin, for the blood of Christ alone under certain circumstances will not avail." (Doctrines of Salvation 1:133)

"But under certain circumstances there are some serious sins for which the cleansing of Christ does not operate, and the law of God is that men must then have their own blood shed to atone for their sins. Murder, for instance, is one of these sins; hence we find the Lord commanding capital punishment. This doctrine can only be practiced in its fullness in a day when the civil and ecclesiastical laws are administered in the same hands." (Mormon Doctrine, *Blood Atonement Doctrine*)

Because of the bloodshed associated with the "cleansing" of the earth, Christ will be dressed in red apparel as he leads his army into battle. His red clothes are a sign of the vengeance he will reap upon the wicked at his coming.[6] Many have been led to believe that it will be when Christ comes in glory to the saints in Zion that He will be dressed in red apparel. But this is clearly not true. The "arm of the Lord" will not fall upon the wicked until long after Christ has come to the faithful saints in Missouri.

"And he was clothed with a vesture dipped in blood: and his name is called The Word of God. And the armies which were in heaven followed him upon white horses, clothed in fine linen, white and clean. And out of his mouth goeth a sharp sword, that with it he should smite the nations: and he shall rule them with a rod of iron; and he treadeth the winepress of the fierceness and wrath of almighty God. And he hath on his vesture and on his thigh a name written, KING OF KINGS, AND LORD OF LORDS." (Revelation 19:13–16)

"And it shall be said: Who is this that cometh down from God in heaven with dyed garments . . . And he shall say: I

---

[6] Isaiah 63:1–4

> *am he who spake in righteousness, mighty to save. And the*
> *Lord shall be red in his apparel, and his garments like him*
> *that treadeth in the wine-vat . . . And his voice shall be*
> *heard: I have trodden the wine-press alone, and have brought*
> *judgment upon all people; and none were with me; And I*
> *have trampled them in my fury, and I did tread upon them in*
> *mine anger, and their blood have I sprinkled upon my gar-*
> *ments, and stained all my raiment; for this was the day of*
> *vengeance which was in my heart." (D&C 133:46–51)*

The description of the blood shed during this period is unprece-
dented. The blood of sinners will flow like wine from a winepress and
become so deep that it will reach the bridles of the horses mounted by
this destroying army, and will cover over 200 square miles of land.

> *"And the angel thrust in his sickle into the earth, and gath-*
> *ered the vine of the earth, and cast it into the great winepress*
> *of the wrath of God. And the winepress was trodden without*
> *the city, and blood came out of the winepress, even unto the*
> *horse bridles, by the space of a thousand and six hundred fur-*
> *longs." (Revelation 14:19–20)*

Along with the destruction being caused by the Army itself, the
Lord will continue to use plagues and natural weapons to destroy the
wicked. What little light from the sun is left to reach the earth, is ex-
tended to protect His army. In fact, just as in the days of Joshua, the
Lord will stop the sun to continue the war without abating. As the
Army of the Anti-Christ realizes that their destruction is inevitable,
they begin to fight among themselves, and finally, flee in panic before
the Lord.[7]

> *"And I will call for a sword against him throughout all my*
> *mountains, saith the Lord God; every man's sword shall be*
> *against his brother. And I will plead against him with pesti-*
> *lence and with blood; and I will rain upon him, and upon his*
> *bands, and upon the many people that are with him, an over-*
> *flowing rain, and great hailstones, fire, and brimstone."*
> *(Ezekiel 38:21–22)*

---

[7] Joshua 10:13; Zechariah 14:5–7; D&C 87:6

"And there fell upon men a great hail out of heaven, every stone about the weight of a talent (about 57 lbs.); and men blasphemed God because of the plague of the hail; for the plague thereof was exceeding great." (Revelation 16:21)

". . . ye shall flee, like as ye fled from before the earthquake in the days of Uzziah king of Judah: and the Lord my God shall come, and all the saints with thee; and it shall come to pass in that day, that the light shall not be clear, nor dark; but it shall be one day which shall be known to the Lord, not day, nor night: but it shall come to pass, that at evening time it shall be light." (Zechariah 14:5–7)

CHRIST ENTERS JERUSALEM

The description of Christ and his army marching into Jerusalem is described in some detail. He will be riding a white horse, and will be wearing clothes that are blood-red in color. As he reaches the Mount of Olives, a great earthquake will cause the mount to divide in two, creating a great valley that permits Christ and his army to directly approach the temple from the east. This earthquake also causes an underground water source to break loose under the temple. This spring of clear water will be used to: 1) cleanse the Temple; 2) permit the Jews who are left alive to be baptized; and 3) flow down to and eventually heal the Dead Sea. The Jews that have survived (only one-third of the Jews that had gathered to Jerusalem are left alive) will rejoice at being rescued. It will be at this time that they finally recognize their Savior, and will be converted and baptized.[8]

And I saw heaven opened, and behold a white horse; and he that sat on him was called Faithful and True, and in righteousness he doth judge and make war. His eyes were as a flame of fire, and on his head were many crowns; and he had a name written, that no man knew, but he himself. And he was clothed with a vesture dipped in blood: and his name was called The Word of God. And the armies which were in

[8] D&C 45:48

83

heaven followed him upon white horses, clothed in fine linen, white and clean." (Revelation 19:11–14)

Then shall the Lord go forth ,and fight against those nations, as when he fought in the day of battle. And his feet shall stand in that day upon the mount of Olives, which is before Jerusalem on the east, and the mount of Olives shall cleave in the midst thereof toward the east and toward the west, and there shall be a very great valley; and half of the mountain shall remove toward the north, and half of it toward the south. And ye shall flee . . . and the Lord my God shall come, and all the saints with thee. And it shall be in that day, that living waters shall go out from Jerusalem; half of them to-ward the former sea, and half of them toward the hinder sea; in summer and in winter shall it be. And the Lord shall be king over all the earth: in that day shall there be one Lord, and his name one." (Zechariah 14:3–8)

The coming of the Lord to Jerusalem, and the earthquakes that occur at that time, will release a spring of water from under the temple. This water is both symbolic of the cleansing of Jerusalem and is actually used to cleanse the temple (desecrated by the Anti-Christ), cleanse the Jews through baptism after their conversion into the true Church, and cleanse the Dead Sea.

Afterward he brought me again unto the door of the house; and, behold, waters issued out from under the threshold of the house eastward. Then said he unto me, these waters issue out toward the east country, and go down into the desert, and go into the sea: which being brought forth into the sea, the waters shall be healed." (Ezekiel 47:1, 8)

"In that day there shall be a fountain opened to the house of David and to the inhabitants of Jerusalem for sin and for un-cleanness." (Zechariah 13:1)

As a final act of humility and repentance, the Jews that are left in Jerusalem will recognize Jesus Christ as the long awaited Messiah and will come to understand that they crucified their Lord and God. As the Jews that are still alive in Jerusalem run to greet the army that saved them from slavery and death, the scene might look similar to Christ's last entrance into Jerusalem more than 2,000 years ago: they will line the streets, cheering and shouting, the exhilaration of the moment overcoming them. Then, slowly, as they come to see the great General that leads this army up close, the truth is suddenly revealed. This great leader is Jesus Christ. The same Jesus that some 2,000 years earlier they had rejected and crucified had now come to save them. We can only imagine the guilt and shame they will feel at that moment, but they will be openly forgiven by the Lord and accepted into the Church and Kingdom of God.[9]

> *"And then shall the Jews look upon me and say: What are these wounds in thine hands and in thy feet? Then shall they know that I am the Lord; for I will say unto them: These wound are the wounds with which I was wounded in the house of my friends. I am he who was lifted up. I am Jesus that was crucified. I am the Son of God. And then shall they weep because of their iniquities; then shall they lament because they persecuted their king." (D&C 45:51–53)*

The Final Plague

After Christ completes the destruction of the army of the Anti-Christ (we are never told what finally happens to the Anti-Christ himself), there is a great plague that is sent to destroy any remaining vestiges of the fleeing army and the wicked that are left alive. Perhaps this is just a continuation of the plague of flies that was caused by the dead bodies left lying in heaps upon the ground, or it may be the after effects of the nuclear and chemical weapons that have been used.

> *"And this shall be the plague wherewith the Lord will smite all the people that have fought against Jerusalem; their flesh shall consume away while they stand upon their feet, and their eyes shall consume away in their holes, and their tongue shall consume away in their mouth." (Zechariah 14:12)*

---

[9] Zechariah 12:9–10, 13:6–9; D&C 133:35; see Note 2

The Supper of the Great God

After the great war is over, the animals and birds gather to a great "supper," to feast upon the dead.[10]

> *"And I saw an angel standing in the sun; and he cried with a loud voice, saying to all the fowls that fly in the midst of heaven, come and gather yourselves together unto the supper of the great God; that ye may eat the flesh of kings, and the flesh of captains, and the flesh of mighty men, and the flesh of horses, and of them that sit on them, and the flesh of all men who fight against the Lamb, both bond and free, both small and great." (Revelation 19:17–18)*

THE WAR'S AFTERMATH

Those left alive after the long war, and those who were righteous enough to remain after Christ's cleansing of the earth, must continue the cleanup of the debris of the war and bury the millions of bodies that remain rotting upon the earth. This will take years, and will be an organized effort directed by the Lord and his leaders. As we have already seen, though Christ came in power and glory He does not do all of the work himself. His followers are part of the army and part of the cleanup of the earth. The earth *will* become a Garden of Eden, a terrestrial state; but it will take a long period of time, and a lot of individual effort.[11]

> *"Behold it is come, and it is done, saith the Lord God; this is the day whereof I have spoken. And they that dwell in the cities of Israel shall go forth, and shall set on fire and burn the weapons, and they shall burn them with fire seven years; so that they shall take no wood out of the field, neither cut down any out of the forests, for they shall burn the weapons with fire. And it shall come to pass in that day, that I will give unto Gog a place there of graves in Israel, the valley of*

---

[10] Ezekiel 39:2, 4
[11] See Note 3

the passengers on the east of the sea: and it shall stop the noses of the passengers: and there shall they bury Gog and all his multitude; and seven months shall the house of Israel be burying of them, that they may cleanse the land. Yea, all the people of the land shall bury them. And they shall separate out men of continual employment, passing through the land to bury with the travelers those that remain upon the face of the earth, to cleanse it: after the end of seven months shall they search. And the travelers that pass through the land, when any seeth a man's bone, then shall he set up a sign by it, till the buriers have buried it in the valley." (Ezekiel 39:8–15)

Just as the cleansing of the earth itself will take a long period of time, the cleansing of the people of the earth will take a long time also. Although all of the "wicked" have been destroyed by the Armies of the Lord, there are still many who deny Christ and refuse to follow him. All of those who are unworthy and/or unable to live on a terrestrial world will either die or be destroyed.

"Those of the terrestrial order will be on the earth during the Millennium but the time must come, as expressed by Zechariah and by Joseph Smith . . . when all the heathens who will not repent must eventually be eliminated from the earth. The sinner being one hundred years old, shall be accursed. We have seen that when Christ comes the wicked, all things corruptible, will be consumed. In other words all that pertains to the telestial kingdom will be removed from the face of the earth." (Joseph Fielding Smith, CHMR, 2:217)

Christ Travels to All Lands, Appears to All People, and Completes the Physical Changes That Will Make the Earth a Terrestrial World

It has been prophesied that when the Lord returns, the earth will become like the Garden of Eden, and return to its paradisiacal glory. To do so, the earth must change from the telestial state it is in now into a terrestrial state.[12] In order to make the Earth like the Garden of Eden, all of the wicked must be destroyed, the land cleansed, and the rest of the people of the earth gathered and organized under the new laws of the Kingdom of God.

At this point in time, most of the wicked have been killed in the long war, and much of the land has been cleansed by the fire that accompanied the army. However, even though the war is over, Christ and his army of faithful Elders must continue their work. Over time, Christ and his followers must visit every part of the earth, cleansing it and physically changing it until the whole earth is clean. In addition, Christ and his representatives call upon all people left alive to obey the laws of the new theocratic government of God and accept Christ as their King.[13]

> *"For behold, he shall stand upon the mount of Olivet, and upon the mighty ocean, even the great deep, and upon the islands of the sea, and upon the land of Zion. And he shall utter his voice out of Zion, and he shall speak from Jerusalem, and his voice shall be heard among all people; and it shall be a voice as the voice of many waters, and as the voice of a great thunder, which shall break down the mountains, and the valleys shall not be found. He shall command the great deep, and it shall be driven back into the north countries, and the islands shall become one land; and the land of Jerusalem and the land of Zion shall be turned back into their own place, and the earth shall be like as it was in the days before it was divided. And the Lord, even the Savior, shall stand in the midst of his people, and shall reign over all flesh."* (D&C 133:20–25)

> *"Christ will appear as the refiner and purifier of both man and beast and all that pertains to this earth, for the earth itself shall undergo a change and receive its former paradisiacal glory."* (Doctrines of Salvation, 3:11)

---

[12] 10th Article of Faith
[13] 2 Nephi 8:3; Note 4

NOTES

1.   Bruce R. McConkie, *Millennial Messiah*, 43:525.

"This time he shall come in flaming fire, the vineyard shall be burned, and every living soul on earth shall know that a new order, of worldwide dimensions, has been ushered in. Thus saith the holy word: 'The Lord Jesus shall be revealed from heaven with his mighty angels, in flaming fire taking vengeance on them that know not God, and that obey not the gospel of our Lord Jesus Christ' (2 Thessalonians. 1:7-8).

"In flaming fire! What kind of fire? Flaming fire is flaming fire. It is actual, literal fire, fire that burns trees, melts ore, and consumes corruption. It is the same kind of fire that burned in the furnace of Nebuchadnezzar when Shadrach, Meshach, and Abednego were cast into its blazing flames. And though the heat and flames of fire 'slew those men' whose lot it was to cast the three Hebrews into its flames, yet, miraculously, upon the bodies of these three 'the fire bad no power, nor was an hair of their head singed, neither were their coats changed, nor the smell of fire had passed on them' (Daniel 3:16-27). And so shall it be at the Second Coming when the same literal fire burns over all the earth. The wicked shall be consumed and the righteous shall be as though they walked in the furnace of Nebuchadnezzar."

2.   Joseph Fielding Smith, *Doctrines of Salvation*, Vol. 3:8.

"JEWS TO BE CONVENED AT SECOND COMING. The Jews in due time will be established in their own land, and the Lord will come, according to his promise, unto his people in the hour of their distress and will deliver them from their enemies. Then will they look upon him and discover his wounds and shall say: 'What are these wounds in thine hands?' And he shall answer them: 'Those with which I was wounded in the house of my friends.' Then will they fall down and worship him as their Redeemer—the Son of God.-8-29 After that they will be cleansed of their sins and shall receive the gospel."

3.   Brigham Young, *Journal of Discourses*, 3:122.

"Is not the unbuilding of the Kingdom of God on earth a temporal labor all the time? It will be built up by physical force and means, by manual labor more than by any particular mental effort of the mind . . . Everything connected with building up Zion requires actual, severe labor. It is nonsense to talk about building up any kingdom except by labor; it requires the labor of every part of our organization, whether it be mental, physical, or spiritual, and that is the only way to build up the Kingdom of God."

4.   Joseph Fielding Smith, *Doctrines of Salvation,* Vol. 3:56.

"EARTH TO BE RENEWED WHEN MILLENNIUM COMES. Latter-day Saints believe that the day is near, even at the doors, when Christ shall make his appearance as the rightful ruler of the earth. When that time comes, the whole earth and all things which remain upon its face shall be changed, and 'the earth will be renewed and receive its paradisiacal glory. That means that the earth shall be brought back to a similar condition which prevailed when peace and righteousness ruled and before death entered with its awful stain of evil and destruction. When that day comes wickedness must cease and every unclean creature shall be swept from the earth for they will not be able to endure the changed conditions.

"All 'element shall melt with fervent heat; and all things shall become new, that my knowledge and glory may dwell upon all the earth. And in that day the enmity of man, and enmity of the beasts, yea, the enmity of all flesh, shall cease from before my face.' Why shall it cease? Because all things upon the face of the earth that are corruptible shall be removed, whether they are men or beasts, they who have wickedness in their hearts cannot stay—they shall be as stubble—they shall be consumed and pass away. And so the earth shall be cleansed that the knowledge of the Lord shall cover the face of the earth."

Chapter Six
The Millennium

The "millennium" officially begins when Christ obtains the keys of power at Adam-ondi-Ahman. From than point on, the church is under the direct control of Jesus Christ and begins to make all the preparations needed to transform the earth into a terrestrial sphere.

As the Saints, under the direction of Jesus Christ their King, work to make the earth like the Garden of Eden, all of society will change. The laws of the U.S. Constitution will be meshed with the Laws of God, and all people will be required to live these laws or be punished—or even destroyed—like the wicked before them. Families will live in peace, raising their children in righteousness. Children will grow up without sin, and at the age of 100 years will not die but will be changed in a twinkling of an eye from mortality to immortality. There will be no more death as we know it. Neither man nor animals will kill for their food, and peace will exist between all life forms. Faith will increase to the point that men will receive everything they ask because they will only ask for what is right.[1]

> "For behold, I create new heavens and a new earth: and the former shall not be remembered, nor come into mind. There shall be no more thence an infant of days, nor an old man

---

[1] Michah 4:3; Isaiah 11:6–9

that hath not filled his days: for the child shall die an hundred years old; but the sinner being an hundred years old shall be accursed. And they shall build houses, and inhabit them; and they shall plant vineyards, and eat the fruit of them. They shall not build, and another inhabit; they shall not plant, and another eat: for as the days of a tree are the days of my people, and mine elect shall long enjoy the work of their hands. The wolf and the lamb shall feed together, and the lion shall eat straw like the bullock: and dust shall be the serpent's meat. They shall not hurt nor destroy in all my holy mountain, saith the Lord." (Isaiah 65:17–25)

"And the earth shall be given unto them for an inheritance; and they shall multiply and wax strong, and their children shall grow up without sin unto salvation." (D&C 45:85)

"And in that day the enmity of man, and the enmity of beasts, yea, the enmity of all flesh, shall cease from before my face. And in that day whatsoever any man shall ask, it shall be given unto him. And in that day Satan shall not have power to tempt any man. And there shall be no sorrow because there is no death. In that day a infant shall not die until he is old; and his life shall be as the age of a tree; and when he dies he shall not sleep, that is to say in the earth, but shall be changed in the twinkling of an eye and shall be caught up, and his rest shall be glorious. Yea, verily I say unto you, in that day when the Lord shall come, he shall reveal all things." (D&C 101:26–32)

After the great wars are over, and after the cleansing of the earth has been completed and life on earth has been transformed into a terrestrial state, Christ and all of the Saints who have been resurrected and prepared for a higher state of existence will leave this earth. This may be new doctrine to some who believe that Christ will live continually on the earth for 1,000 years, but we must remember that Christ has many, many worlds for which He is responsible, and He will come and go as those responsibilities require. In addition, the Saints that have been resurrected as Celestial beings are not required to wait, but are permitted to leave this earth in order to continue their progression and live on a Celestial world. They will be permitted to leave this earth to follow their dreams and fortunes in the Celestial worlds already created. They will leave to begin their own eternal families and create their own eternal worlds.

> "*It would be inconsistent for mortals and immortals to dwell together. The resurrected Saints and Christ will visit as Christ did with his disciples for forty days after his resurrection. Their natural abode, however, must be on some celestial world until this world is finally celestialized.*" (Joseph Fielding Smith, CHMR, 2:217)

> "*Jesus has been upon the earth a great many more times than you are aware of . . . Will he remain and dwell upon the earth a thousand years, without returning? He will come here, and return to his mansions where he dwells with his Father, and come again to the earth, and again return to his Father, according to my understanding.*" (Brigham Young, Journal of Discourses, 7:142)

Although all of the wicked have been destroyed and the earth itself is now in a terrestrial state of existence, it will be possible for men to sin during the Millennium because they will still have their agency. However, because of the presence of the Lord almost all men will choose to do good. Satan will have no power because the people of the earth will not have the desire to do evil. Those few who continue to sin will be punished, and if they refuse to repent they will be put to death, just like the wicked before them.

> "*Will it be possible for men to sin during the Millennium? Yes. Why? Because they have not lost their agency. The Lord will not destroy the agency of the people during the Millennium, therefore there will be a possibility of their sinning during that time.*" (Orson Pratt, Journal of Discourses, 16:318)

> "*And because of the righteousness of his people, Satan has no power; wherefore, he cannot be loosed for the space of many years; for he hath no power over the hearts of the people, for they dwell in righteousness, and the Holy One of Israel reigneth.*" (1 Nephi 22:26)

"And it shall come to pass that every one that is left of all the nations which came against Jerusalem shall even go up from year to year to worship the King, the Lord of hosts, and to keep the feast of tabernacles. And it shall be, that whoso will not come up of all the families of the earth unto Jerusalem to worship the King, the Lord of hosts, even upon them shall be no rain." (Zechariah 14:16–17)

As hard as it is to believe, there will be people who choose to believe in and follow different religions during the Millennium. The only requirement for living during the Millennium will be to keep the laws and commandments of the government of God. Just as now, anyone (even nonbelievers) will be permitted to participate in the government. While continuing to protect the rights of all people to believe and think as they choose, missionary work will continue until the entire world is converted and baptized by those having the proper authority.

"When the Kingdom of Heaven spreads over the whole earth, do you expect that all the people composing the different nations will become Latter-day Saints? If you do, you will be much mistaken . . . there will be every sort of sect and party, and every individual what he supposes to be the best in religion, and in everything else, similar to what it is now."
(Brigham Young, Journal of Discourses, 2:316)

"People will enter the great reign of Jesus Christ carrying with them their beliefs and religious doctrines. Their agency will not be taken from them. In the millennium men will have the privilege of their own belief, but they will not have the privilege of treating the name and character of Deity as they have done heretofore. No, but every knee shall bow and every tongue confess to the glory of God the Father that Jesus is the Christ. The Prophet Joseph Smith has said: 'There will be wicked men on the earth during the thousand years. The heathen nations who will not come up to worship will be visited with the judgments of God, and must eventually be destroyed from the earth.' The gospel will be taught far more intensely and with greater power during the millennium, until all the inhabitants of the earth shall

94

embrace it. Eventually all people will embrace the truth." (Doctrines of Salvation 3:63)

"The Kingdom grows out of the Church, but it is not the Church, for a man may be a legislator in that body which will issue laws to sustain the inhabitants of the earth in their individual rights, and still not belong to the Church of Jesus Christ at all." (Brigham Young, Journal of Discourses, 2:310)

Almost everything about society as we know it will change. We will change our lives to adapt to the laws and lifestyle of a terrestrial world. Everything from the language we speak to the food we eat must change. Everyone will learn a new language, as eventually there will only be one language spoken—the same language that was spoken by Adam and Eve in the Garden of Eden. All people and animals will have to become vegetarians because there will be no more death as we know it.

"For then will I turn to the people a pure language, that they may all call upon the name of the Lord, to serve him with one consent." (Zephaniah 3:9)

"Implicit in this pronouncement is the fact that man and all forms of life will be vegetarians in the coming day; and the eating of meat will cease, because for one thing, death as we know it ceases. There will be no more shedding of blood, because man and beast are changed (quickened) and blood no longer flows in their veins." (Millennial Messiah, p. 658)

One of the great blessings that will come during the millennium will be opportunity to read about mysteries hidden since the foundation of the world. The time will come when the Lord will reveal all things to the Saints, and all of the sealed portions of the scriptures will be translated and published.

" . . . the brass plates will also come forth in due time as part of the restoration of all things, the sealed portion of the Book of Mormon will not come forth until after the Lord Jesus comes." (Millennial Messiah, p. 113)

Polygamy will be reinstated as a law because of the lack of men left alive on earth, and because the Saints will be required to live this law in the Celestial Kingdom. Most priesthood holders who have held positions of authority in the Church understand and accept there will be more women in the Celestial Kingdom than men. Women are naturally more spiritual than men. Because of this spiritual disparity, and in order to give all women the opportunity to live in the highest degree of the Celestial Kingdom, the Celestial law of polygamy will have to be lived.

> *"In that day family units will be perfected according to the plans made in the heavens before the peopling of the earth. Celestial marriage in its highest and most glorious form will bind men and women together in eternal unions, and the resultant families will truly continue forever. One of the most provocative millennial passages forecasts the order of matrimony that will then prevail, saying: 'And in that day (the millennial day) seven women shall take hold of one man, saying, we will eat our own bread, and wear our own apparel: only let us be called by thy name, to take away our reproach' (the reproach of being without a husband, without children, without a family of their own). This shall come to pass after the destruction of the wicked, and it is one of many scriptural intimations that the generality of women are more spiritual than are most men. And they, being clean and upright, and desiring family units and children and the exaltation that grows out of all these things, will turn to the marriage discipline of Abraham their father so they may be blessed like Sarah of old."* (Millennial Messiah, p. 113)

The concept of plural marriage has always been one of the most difficult doctrines to understand and accept. However, all men and women must come to terms with this doctrine and be able to live it. The eternal consequences of doing otherwise will put them at risk of losing their salvation.

> *"God never introduced the Patriarchal order of marriage (polygamy) with a view to please man in his carnal desires,*

> *nor to punish females for anything which they had done; but*
> *He introduced it for the express purpose of raising up to His*
> *name a royal Priesthood, a peculiar people. Do not reject*
> *anything because it is new or strange, and do not sneer nor*
> *jeer at what comes from the Lord, for if we do, we endanger*
> *our salvation."* (Brigham Young, Journal of Discourses,
> 3:264)

Another of the great blessings that will come during the millennium will be that all of the righteous will obtain their Calling and Election, and will have the opportunity to enter the temples of God and be sealed to eternal life.

> *"And all of the faithful will have their callings and elections*
> *made sure and will be sealed up unto that eternal life which*
> *will come to them when they reach the age of a tree. (100*
> *years old)"* (Millennial Messiah, p. 674)

During the 1,000 year millennial era several events will occur that are of some importance. These milestones in the progress of the Kingdom of God are heralded by the sounds of trumpets.

THE SECOND TRUMP

Long after the Millennium has begun, the first resurrection will continue. Remember, the first resurrection has at least two parts: 1) the "morning" of the first resurrection when the Church of the Firstborn (the righteous Saints) and those who are the leadership of the church are resurrected; and 2) the general resurrection when the Heathen Nations and those who are of at least a "terrestrial" nature will be resurrected. The second trump is a sign of the completion of the resurrection of the Church of the Firstborn, and the start of this first general resurrection.

> *"And after this another angel shall sound, which is the second trump; and then cometh the redemption of those who are Christ's at his coming; who have received their part in that*

> prison which is prepared for them, that they might receive
> the gospel, and be judged according to men in the
> flesh." (D&C 88:99)

> "And then shall the heathen nations be redeemed, and they
> that knew no law shall have part in the first resurrection;
> and it shall be tolerable for them." (D&C 45:54)

> "After the Lord and the righteous who are caught up to meet
> him have descended upon the earth, there will come to pass
> another resurrection. In this resurrection will come forth
> those of the terrestrial order, who were not worthy to be
> caught up to meet him, but who are worthy to come forth to
> enjoy the millennial reign. This other class are those who are
> not members of the Church of the Firstborn, but who have led
> honorable lives, although they refused to accept the fullness
> of the gospel. Also in this class will be numbered those who
> died without law and hence are not under condemnation for
> a violation of the commandments of the Lord." (Doctrines of
> Salvation, 2:296)

When a person is resurrected, the body and spirit are united in a
final and permanent state. Therefore, we can assume that people who
are in the spirit world will wait until they have reached their
"ultimate" eternal progression before being resurrected—since once
they are resurrected they will no longer be able to progress to a higher
level. This is one of the reasons that the first resurrection will take so
long. Missionaries will continue to preach the gospel on earth and in
the spirit world, and Saints on earth will continue to complete the
temple work necessary for people to obtain the Celestial Kingdom of
God.

> "In the resurrection there will be different kinds of bodies;
> they will not all be alike. Bodies will be quickened according
> to the kingdom which they are judged worthy to enter. There
> will be several classes of resurrected bodies; some celestial,
> some terrestrial, some telestial, and some sons of perdition.
> There will be some physical peculiarity by which each indi-
> vidual in every class can be identified." (Doctrines of Sal-
> vation 2:286)

Another factor in the "process" of the resurrection, is that those who will eventually obtain the Celestial Kingdom must have their temple work done *prior* to being resurrected. Much of the work the Saints will be doing in the Millennium will be temple work for the dead. Once the temple work has been done, those Saints who are waiting can be resurrected. Only after all the temple work for the dead is completed will the first resurrection be completed.

> During the thousand years of peace the great work of the Lord shall be in the temples, and into those temples the people shall go to labor for those who have passed beyond and who are waiting to have these ordinances which pertain to their salvation performed for them by those who still dwell in mortality upon the earth." (Doctrines of Salvation, 3:58)

THE THIRD TRUMP

The third trump signals a judgment that is made upon the wicked. Those who are not worthy to be resurrected and live with Christ during the Millennium (those who have refused to repent), must stay in Hell (or in Spirit Prison) for a thousand years.[2] In addition, we should assume that there will be some who sin during the Millennial period. As all men will still have their agency, there will surely be a few who choose to sin, who choose to disobey the laws set up by the government of God. If they do not repent, or if the sin is serious in nature, they will be put to death, just as the wicked before them. They then will have to live with the other wicked spirits in Hell until the end of the Millennium. In this way the earth will remain clean for the duration of the thousand years.

> "And again, another trump shall sound, which is the third trump; and then come the spirits of men who are to be judged, and are found under condemnation; and these are the rest of the dead; and they live not again until the thousand

---

[2] D&C 133:64–73

years are ended, neither again, until the end of the earth."
(D&C 88:100)

"And again, we saw the glory of the telestial, they who received not the gospel of Christ, neither the testimony of Jesus. These are they who shall not be redeemed from the devil until the last resurrection." (D&C 76:81–85)

"It is decreed that the unrighteous shall have to spend their time during this thousand years in the prison house prepared for them where they can repent and cleanse themselves through the things which they shall suffer." (Doctrines of Salvation, 3:60)

THE FOURTH TRUMP

The fourth trump signals the time when all those who are still on earth are living a terrestrial lifestyle and have rejected Satan. A judgment is made upon Satan and the Sons of Perdition: they are bound for one thousand years due to the righteousness of the people.[3]

"And another trump shall sound, which is the fourth trump, saying: there are found among those who are to remain until that great and last day, even the end, who shall remain filthy still." (D&C 88:102)

"And I saw an angel come down from heaven, having the key of the bottomless pit and a great chain in his hand. And he laid hold on the dragon, that old serpent, which is the Devil, and Satan, and bound him a thousand years." (Revelation 20:1–2)

THE FIFTH TRUMP

The fifth trump sounds, signaling the time when the Kingdom of God and its laws have established control over the entire earth. All

---

[3] D&C 29:11, 43:31, 45:55

nations and all people have personally accepted Jesus Christ as their King, and have covenanted to obey the laws and commandments of this new Kingdom. The gospel of Jesus Christ continues to be preached to all people in an effort to convert the whole world.[4]

> *"And another trump shall sound, which is the fifth trump, which is the angel who committeth the everlasting gospel – – flying through the midst of heaven, unto all nations, kindreds, tongues, and people; for every ear shall hear it, and every knee shall bow, and every tongue shall confess; for the hour of his judgment is come." (D&C 88:103)*

THE SIXTH TRUMP

As we near the end of the Millennium, the sixth trump signals the time when all people living on the earth are converted to the gospel of Jesus Christ. The great Abominable Church (the false doctrines taught by other churches) has finally been defeated by the persuasion of truth.[5]

> *"And again, another angel shall sound his trump, which is the sixth angel, saying: she is fallen who made all nations drink of the wine of the wrath of her fornication; she is fallen, is fallen!" (D&C 88:105)*

THE SEVENTH TRUMP

The seventh trump signals the completion of the work of the righteous, and the triumph of Jesus Christ. The entire world has been converted to the Church of Jesus Christ; all temple work for the dead has been completed; and all of the righteous (both Celestial and terrestrial) have been resurrected.[6]

---

[4] Mosiah 16:1, 27:31
[5] See Note 1
[6] D&C 88:108–110

"And again, another angel shall sound his trump, which is the seventh angel, saying: It is finished; it is finished! The Lamb of God hath overcome and trodden the wine-press alone, even the wine-press of the fierceness of the wrath of Almighty God. And then shall the angels be crowned with the glory of his might, and the saints shall be filled with his glory, and receive their inheritance and be made equal with him." (D&C 88:106)

NOTES

1. *Doctrines of Salvation,* Vol. 3:64

"SPREAD OF GOSPEL DURING MILLENNIUM. The gospel will be taught far more intensely and with greater power during the millennium, until all the inhabitants of the earth shall embrace it. Satan shall be bound so that he cannot tempt any man. Should any man refuse to repent and accept the gospel under those conditions then he would be accursed. Through the revelations given to the prophets, we learn that during the reign of Jesus Christ for a thousand years eventually all people will embrace the truth."

Chapter Seven
The Final Trump and the End of the Millennium

The time will come when the rest of the dead must be resurrected. These are the wicked people who were not worthy to live on the earth during the millennium and are still living in Spirit Prison or Hell. Since the only people who have not been resurrected at this time are the most wicked, their resurrection will have a profound effect upon the earth and the society then living. Just picture it: millions upon millions of evil, wicked people, resurrected to live again upon the earth. Satan will be free again to tempt the children of God. The earth and its society will be transformed—once again—into a telestial state, subject to disease, pain, and corruption.[1]

> "But behold, before the earth shall pass away, Michael, mine archangel, shall sound his trump, and then shall all the dead awake, for their graves shall be opened, and they shall come forth – yea, even all." (D&C 29:26)

The resurrection of the wicked is the event that brings an end to the 1,000 year Millennial period and Christ's personal reign upon earth.

---

[1] D&C 76:82, 84–85, 103–106, 109

Many who were born and raised during the millennium will fall into temptation and sin for the very first time. If they do sin and fall from grace, they will become Sons of Perdition. Anyone and everyone who follows Satan during this period will become Sons of Perdition because they will all have a perfect knowledge of the gospel and of Jesus Christ and yet willfully turn from that light and knowledge to follow Satan.[2]

> "When the period called the Millennium has passed away, Satan will again be loosed . . . unnumbered millions of the posterity of those who lived during the Millennium will be scattered in the four quarters of the earth, and Satan will go forth and tempt them, and overcome some of them, so that they will rebel against God; not rebel in ignorance, but they will sin willfully against the law of heaven, and so great will the power of Satan be over them, that he will gather them together against the Saints and against the beloved city, and fire will come down out of heaven and consume them."
> (Orson Pratt, Journal of Discourses, 16:322)

> "During the Millennium, Satan is bound. Because of the righteousness of the people, he has no power over them...but, men will begin again, gradually, to partake of the things of this world; pride and carnality and crime will commence anew; true believers will be persecuted and false churches will arise. Satan will be loosed because he is no longer bound by the righteousness of the people." (Millennial Messiah, p. 694)

The period of time that Satan will be loosed will last about one thousand years. The scriptures teach that the Savior came in the "meridian of time." We are told that Christ's birth came at the beginning of the fourth thousand year of time since Adam; this then would make the full period of earth's time to be eight thousand years. The end of the millennium would be the start of this final thousand years of time.

---

[2] Mosiah 3:20–21

> *"And again, verily, verily, I say unto you that when the thousand years are ended, and men again begin to deny their God, then will I spare the earth but for a little season."* (D&C 29:22)

> *"This 'little season' is presumed to be another thousand years."* (Millennial Messiah, p. 695)

It will be some time during this "little season" that the wombs of women on earth will be closed, and no more children will be born. This will be because all of the spirits destined to live upon this earth will have obtained their physical bodies. From this time no more children will be born until after the earth is made a Celestial world.

> *"Until the last spirit that has been designed to come here and take a tabernacle has come upon the earth, the winding-up scene cannot come."* (Brigham Young, Journal of Discourses, 8:352)

Remember, all of this time the earth has been traveling through space towards Kolob. As it nears the great center of the universe, the light from other celestial planets and suns will light its way. During periods of darkness in the void of space, the earth has had its own source of light—Jesus Christ.

We know very little about this period of time. Will the people of the earth continue to be subject to death, and therefore need another resurrection? Will the church and kingdom continue, requiring Prophets and Apostles? We just don't know. We do know, however, that at the end of this thousand years a great war will take place—a second Armageddon—called the "Battle of the Great God." As seen before upon the earth, the righteous and wicked will naturally migrate to separate areas of the earth. Then there will be one final battle to obtain control of the earth. The difference in this war will be that the wicked will be destroyed by a Celestial fire—the same fire that will bring about the final transformation of the earth, changing it from a terrestrial sphere into a Celestial world.[3]

---

[3] D&C 29:22–29

> *"And then he (Satan) shall be loosed for a little season, that he may gather together his armies. And Michael, the seventh angel, even the archangel, shall gather together his armies, even the hosts of heaven. And the devil shall gather together his armies; even the hosts of hell, and shall come up to battle against Michael and his armies. And then cometh the battle of the great God; and the devil and his armies shall be cast away into their own place, that they shall not have power over the saints any more at all. For Michael shall fight their battles, and shall overcome him who seeketh the throne of him who sitteth upon the throne, even the Lamb." (D&C 88:111–115)*

> *"And when the thousand years are expired, Satan shall be loosed out of his prison, and shall go out to deceive the nations which are in the four quarters of the earth, Gog and Magog, to gather them together to battle: the number of whom is as the sand of the sea. And they went up on the breadth of the earth, and compassed the camp of the saints about, and the beloved city: and fire came down from God out of heaven, and devoured them. And the devil that deceived them was cast into the lake of fire and brimstone, where the beast and the false prophet are, and shall be tormented day and night for ever and ever." (Revelation 20:7)*

It will be during this final battle that the wicked, including Satan and the Sons of Perdition, will be destroyed. This destruction will come in two stages. First, as the Celestial fire consumes the earth, it will destroy the physical bodies of the wicked, even and including the bodies of the resurrected Sons of Perdition. The Sons of Perdition (those spirits that had obtained bodies and then committed the unpardonable sin of murder) will have been resurrected with the rest of the wicked at the end of the millennium. However, because they continue to choose to follow Satan, they will suffer a "second death," a second separation of the body and spirit. They will become spirits again to be like, with, and subject to their lord and master: Satan. Then Satan and all of the evil "spirits" that follow him will be destroyed.

The second stage of this process will consist of the destruction of the spirit bodies of the wicked. Since all of the wicked are now spirits (Satan, his angels, and the Sons of Perdition are all existing together as spirits), they are prepared to suffer their final fate together. This final act of destruction will come in the form of a bottomless pit (akin to a black hole in the Universe), a place and process that will actually reverse all of the progression made by these spirits. It will mean that Satan, his angels, and all of the Sons of Perdition that followed him will pass through this bottomless pit and become what they once were—simple intelligences.[4]

> "If I do not live my religion, but turn away from the principles of light and life, my spirit will die. There are thousands upon thousands whose bodies will die by the power of the 'second death;' and then they never will return again. Many call that annihilation. God will make a desolation of those bodies and spirits, and he will throw them back into the earth; that is, that portion that belongs to the earth will go back there. And so it will be with our spirits: they will go back into the elements or space that they once occupied before they came here." (Heber C. Kimball, Journal of Discourses, 5:271)

> "The second death is the dissolution of the organized particles which compose the spirit, and their return to their native element." (Brigham Young, Journal of Discourses, 9:147)

The rest of the wicked will be given homes on worlds suited to their love of darkness, while the Saints prepare to live on worlds of light.

> "Is it possible then, that there are worlds reserved in eternal night, in an eternal eclipse, rolling in the shade? What is their use? They are the homes of them that love darkness rather then light; and it shall be said unto them, depart, ye cursed, into outer darkness. There are planets that revolve in eternal darkness, that you who love darkness rather than

---

[4] JST Matthew 1:4; 2 Peter 3:7, 10, 13; Jude 1:6, 13

> *light may go and find your own home. There is a place pre-*
> *pared for every body, no matter what their character."*
> *(Orson Hyde,* Journal of Discourses, *1:130)*

The earth is cleansed by fire at the same time the wicked are destroyed. When this final cleansing is finished the earth will become a celestial world, completing its final preparation to become the abode of celestial beings. The earth is a living thing, and as such will die and be resurrected—changed into an immortal, celestial, living world. Then this celestial earth and its celestial people will take their place among the other celestial worlds at the center of the universe. The great gathering of worlds will be completed, and the final judgment will begin.[5]

> *"And I saw a new heaven and a new earth: for the first*
> *heaven and the first earth were passed away; and there was*
> *no more sea." (Revelation 21:1)*

> *"Every creature on the earth, whether it be man, animal,*
> *fish, fowl, or other creature, that the Lord has created, is re-*
> *deemed from death on the same terms that man is redeemed.*
> *The earth itself shall be changed from its mortal body, for it*
> *too is a living thing now, under curse of death, and it*
> *'abideth the law of a celestial kingdom, for it filleth the meas-*
> *ure of its creation, and transgresseth not the law – wherefore*
> *it shall be sanctified, yea, notwithstanding it shall die, it*
> *shall be quickened again.'"* (Doctrines of Salvation, 2:281)

> *"And before the throne there was a sea of glass like unto*
> *crystal." (Revelation 4:6)*

> *"What is the sea of glass spoken of by John? It is the earth, in*
> *its sanctified, immortal, and eternal state." (D&C 77:1)*

> *"The angels do not reside on a planet like this earth; but they*
> *reside in the presence of God, on a globe like a sea of glass*
> *and fire, where all things for their glory are manifest, past,*

---

[5] 1 Nephi 22:17; 3 Nephi 26:3; D&C 101:24–25

present, and future, and are continually before the Lord. The place where God resides is a great Urim and Thummim. This earth, in its sanctified and immortal state, will be made like unto crystal and will be a Urim and Thummim to the inhabitants who dwell thereon, whereby all things pertaining to an inferior kingdom, be manifest to those who dwell on it; and this earth will be Christ's." (D&C 130:6–9)

NOTES

1. *Doctrines of Salvation,* Vol. 3:64.

"SPREAD OF GOSPEL DURING MILLENNIUM. The gospel will be taught far more intensely and with greater power during the millennium, until all the inhabitants of the earth shall embrace it. Satan shall be bound so that he cannot tempt any man. Should any man refuse to repent and accept the gospel under those conditions then he would be accursed. Through the revelations given to the prophets, we learn that during the reign of Jesus Christ for a thousand years eventually all people will embrace the truth."

Conclusion

All believers in Jesus Christ look forward to the time he will come again. To the saints (members of The Church of Jesus Christ of Latter-day Saints), that time will come at the sacred meeting held at Adam-ondi-Ahman, when all worthy members will witness and participate in the sustaining of Jesus Christ as head of the Kingdom of God on earth. To the righteous members of other churches, it will be when Christ returns in glory. The events that lead up to Christ's coming, and the transformation that will occur afterward, will be real. It will not be "spiritual" in nature, but temporal and physical and real.

> *"And now behold, I, Nephi, say unto you that all these things must come according to the flesh." (1 Nephi 22:27)*

The faithful Saints living on the earth at the time of Christ's coming will *know* ahead of time when He will come and what they will need to do to prepare for His arrival. They will *know* because they have watched for and seen the signs, and they will *know* because it will be revealed to the living prophet of God, and he, in turn, will lead them to safety.

> *"Surely the Lord God will do nothing, until he revealeth his secret unto his servants the prophets." (Amos 2:7, JST)*

Those who are prepared for his coming will not fear these events, but will look forward to them. Their faith will cast out all fear, and their faith will protect them. By understanding and looking for the signs of Christ's coming we will all be prepared for that day.

Bibliography

Ballard, Melvin J. General Conference Report, April, 1925.

Capt, E. Raymond. *The Resurrection Tomb.*

Cannon, George Q. *Gospel Truth.*

Ehat, Andrew F. and Lyndon W. Cook. *The Words of Joseph Smith.*

Encyclopedia Americana, 1990.

Jessee, Dean. *The John Taylor Journal.*

The Journal of Discourses Volumes 1–26.

Kimball, Heber C., *The Life of Heber C. Kimball.*

Letter from Pontius Pilate to Tiberius Caesar, Congressional Library, Washington, DC.

Mackay, David O. *BYU Speeches 5/10/61.*

Mackay, David O. *Gospel Ideals.*

Maxwell, Neal A. *But for a Small Moment.*

McConkie, Bruce R. *Doctrinal New Testament Commentary.*

McConkie, Bruce R. *Mormon Doctrine.*

McConkie, Bruce R. *The Promised Messiah.*

McConkie, Bruce R. *The Millennial Messiah.*

McIntosh, Dr. and Dr. Twyman. *The Archko Volume,* from manuscripts in Constantinople and *The records of the Senatorial Docket, the Vatican of Rome,* Antiquarian Lodge.

Pratt, Parley, *The Angel of the Prairies.*

Roberts, B. H. *New Witness for God.*

Smith, Joseph. *History of the Church of Jesus Christ of Latter-day Saints.*

Smith, Joseph. *Holy Bible, Joseph Smith Translation.*

Smith, Joseph Fielding. *Church History and Modern Revelation.*

Smith, Joseph Fielding. *Doctrines of Salvation.*

Smith, Joseph Fielding. *Teachings of the Prophet Joseph Smith.*

Smith, Joseph Fielding. *The Way to Perfection.*

The Standard Works: *The Book of Mormon: Another Testament of Jesus Christ, The Doctrine of Covenants, The Holy Bible, The Pearl of Great Price.*

Talmage, James E. *The Articles of Faith.*

Talmage, James E. *Jesus the Christ*

Taylor, John. *The Gospel Kingdom.*

Tuchman, Barbara. *The Bible and the Sword.*

Velikovsky, Immanuel. *Worlds in Collision.*

Widtsoe, John A. *Evidences and Reconciliations.*

Scriptural References

Restoration of the Gospel/Times of the Gentiles Begin

D&C 45:28	When times of gentiles come gospel breaks forth
D&C 45:30	In that generation times of the gentiles fulfilled
D&C 88:44	Elders sent among gentiles for the last time
D&C 109:60	Early church identified with the gentiles
D&C 133:5–8	Missionaries sent to all nations; gentiles first, then Jews
D&C 133:10	Missionary cry: Christ is coming, prepare
2 Nephi 15:13	Fullness of gospel to gentiles first, then through them to Israel
2 Nephi 27:1	Last days equals days of the gentiles
Ether 4:17	Book of Mormon to come forth in last days
Doc of Sal 3:10	Joseph Smith messenger before the Lord's coming
Malachi 3:1	Will send a messenger to prepare the way; the Lord will suddenly come to His temple
Romans 11:25	Blindness in Israel until Times of Gentiles is come in

Note: About 100 years after the restoration, the nation of Israel was established.

The Establishment of Zion

Article of Faith 10	Zion/New Jerusalem built in America
D&C 29:8	Called to gather to one place on this land
D&C 45:64	Gather from the east, go west to New Jerusalem
D&C 45:69	Zion only people not at war
D&C 45:70	Nations of the earth afraid to war against Zion
D&C 49:24–25	Before Christ comes Lamanites blossom, Zion flourish, are assembled together at the appointed place
D&C 57:2–3	Center place of Zion is Jackson County, Missouri
D&C 84:2	Mount Zion is the New Jerusalem
D&C 84:4	New Jerusalem begins at building of first temple

D&C 101:77–80	Constitution established by God to protect freedom, the church, will be in place forever
D&C 103:4	Opportunity to build Zion lost due to sin
D&C 103:16	Man like Moses raised up to lead people to Zion, Brigham Young
D&C 105:9	Due to sin must wait for redemption of Zion
D&C 109:73	Church comes forth out of darkness, terrible as an army
D&C 124:26–28	Reestablishment of Zion in Nauvoo by building temple
D&C 125:2	Many cities to be built as part of Zion
D&C 133:12–13	Gentiles gather to Zion, Jews to Jerusalem
1 Nephi 22:7	Lord to raise up a mighty gentile nation on this land
2 Nephi 10:10–14	Land of liberty, fortified against all nations, he that fights against Zion will perish
2 Nephi 10:19	America consecrated to Israel forever
3 Nephi 20:22	This people to be established in this land, called New Jerusalem
Isaiah 2:2–5	Mountain of the Lord established in top of the mountains
Isaiah 5:26	Will lift up an ensign to the nations
Isaiah 11:10–12	Joseph Smith to develop the ensign
Isaiah 603-5	Gentiles come to thy light, their wealth to flow unto Israel
Daniel 2:35, 44	Stone cut out of a mountain to fill the whole earth, will destroy all other nations
TPJS 79	Center place of Zion is Jackson County, Missouri
TPJS 161	Only Zion and her stakes to have peace
TPJS 362	All of America is Zion
History 5:85	Saints to be driven to Rocky Mountains
JD 20:318	Those who won't fight flee to Zion, i.e., WWI, WWIII, emigration
Doc of Sal 2:246	New Jerusalem temple to be built in Jackson County, Zion
Doc of Sal 3:72	Center place of New Jerusalem in Jackson County, same place as Garden of Eden; Zion is America

America (Zion) is cleansed

D&C 45:31	Overflowing scourge and sickness covers the land
D&C 45:63	War is at your doors, soon war in your own land
TPJS 17	US to have scene of bloodshed to sweep wicked off the land; Civil War. This war is to prepare Zion (America) for the return of the lost tribes from the north countries (emigration from Europe)
TPJS 161	Only Zion and her stakes to have peace (no war in America)
History 1:316	Scene of bloodshed in US (Civil War) to cleans wicked to prepare for return of the lost tribes from north countries (Europe)

Period of Preparatory Wars

D&C 87:2	War poured out upon all nations, beginning with Civil War
D&C 87:6	Eventually, war will make an end of all nations
1 Nephi 14:16	Wars among all nations belonging to abominable church
1 Nephi 14:17	Wars are to prepare nations to fulfill covenants of the Lord
1 Nephi 22:13–14	All nations (abominable church) that fight against house of Israel (Zion) will turn against one another and war among themselves
Doc of Sal 3:17	The destroying angels have been set loose (1893)
History 1:23	Wars and rumors of war, end is not yet
JD 7:186	Two periods of warfare, the first to prepare countries to receive the gospel; the second, wars of destruction
Mil Mess 138	Lord to use war to open doors to preach the gospel

Note: WWI and WWII a result of the gentile nations rejecting the gospel, and to prepare the conditions for the establishment of the nation of Israel

Nation of Israel Established (Times of the Gentiles fulfilled)

Article of Faith 10	Literal gathering of Israel, restoration of the ten tribes
D&C 45:25	Jews scattered until Times of the Gentiles fulfilled
D&C 45:43	Before coming, a remnant gathered to this place (Israel)
D&C 49:24–25	Lamanites to blossom as a rose
D&C 109:62–64	Jerusalem to be redeemed from this hour, Jews to return (1836)
2 Nephi 30:7	Jews begin to believe in Christ
Ether 13:5	Jerusalem to be rebuilt unto the house of Israel
Isaiah 19:16–17	Judah becomes powerful in politics and war
Isaiah 49:22–23	Lord to lift up gentiles, who will save and restore Israel
Isaiah 60:5	Wealth of gentiles to flow unto Israel
Isaiah 60:10	Sons of strangers shall build up thy walls (gentiles)
Isaiah 60:16	Suck milk of gentiles suck breast of Kings
Ezekiel 36:24	Israel gathered to their own land
Ezekiel 37:22	There shall be one nation and one king in Israel
Zechariah 1:16–17	Jerusalem established as capital city
Luke 21:24	Jerusalem trodden down until Times of Gentiles fulfilled
Doc of Sal 3:8	Jews begin to believe in Christ, after Times of Gentiles
Conf Report Apr 1960	We may now say the Jews have returned to Palestine, the nation of Israel reborn (George Q. Morris)
Church News 1931	The day of down-trodden Israel is now at hand, the sign for the fulfillment of this prophesy has been given (Joseph F. Smith)

Revelation on the Priesthood (Times of the Jews fulfilled)

D&C 90:9–10	After gospel sent to gentiles and Jews, given to heathen nations
Moses 7:8, 22	Mark of Cain is black skin
Abraham 1:21–27	Curse of Cain is not being able to hold the priesthood
JD 7:290	Gospel given to Negroes last, after all other people

Solomon's Temple Rebuilt

Zechariah 6:12–15	They that are far off shall come to build temple
Revelations 11:1	The apostle John to initiate building of temple
Daniel 9:24–25	From building of temple to coming of Christ is 69 weeks
History 6:253	New leader, David, helps rebuild temple
TPJS 286	Jerusalem rebuilt and the temple
Mil Mess 279	Temple to be rebuilt by LDS church
Mil Mess 448	Temple will be focal point of final war

Note: David Ben Gurian was leader that helped establish Israel

The Anti-Christ Comes to Power

Daniel 7:19–26	The horn (king) to prevail against saints until Ancient of days comes; He will change laws and time for 3 1/2 years
Daniel 8:23–25	Evil king comes to power and has ability to destroy, shall prosper, and cause people to do evil
2 Thess 2:2–4	Christ not come until a falling away, son of perdition revealed; he opposes God, will sit in temple and say he is God
2 Thes 2:7–9 JST	Christ suffers Satan to work, Christ will consume Satan at His coming; until then Satan deceives with all power, signs and lying wonder
Revelation 9:11	Ruler called the destroyer
Revelation 16:14–16	False prophets perform miracles, persuade nations to go to war against Israel
Revelation 17:12, 17	Ten nations to follow the beast
Revelation 19:19	The beast to make war against Christ
History 1:22	False prophets show great signs and wonders
JD 7:189	Three false prophets perform miracles

World Rejects Gospel/Missionaries Called Home

D&C 45:26	Wars, whole earth in commotion
D&C 45:27	Love of men wax cold
2 Nephi 27:1	All nations wicked and drunk with iniquity
History 1:30	Love of men wax cold
JD 8:123	After gospel to world, and is rejected, missionaries are called home

Doc of Sal 3:2	Lord comes when earth is ripe in iniquity
Mil Mess 143	When saints have done all they can, the Lord takes over

US Government Falls

JD 6:152	When constitution in danger, elders will save
JD 7:15	Destiny of nation hangs by a thread, saints save
JD 12:344	New York earthquake, Boston tidal wave, Albany fire (August 22, 1863)
JD 13:126	Constitution to be incorporated into Kingdom of God
JD 20:151	US destroyed by internal wars
Doc of Sal 3:13	All governments will fall

New Jerusalem

Article of Faith 10	Zion/New Jerusalem built in America
D&C 49:25	Before Christ comes, saints gather at appointed place
D&C 101:18	The faithful shall return to build up Zion
D&C 103:15–19	Redemption of Zion by power, man like Moses leads
D&C 133:2	Lord shall suddenly come to his temple (in America)
D&C 133:4	Gather to Zion and sanctify yourselves
D&C 133:18	Lamb shall stand on Mount Zion with 144,000 (in America)
Moses 7:62	Elect gathered to prepare holy city, Zion, New Jerusalem
Ether 13:3	New Jerusalem will be in America, to come down from heaven (City of Enoch)
Ether 13:6, 8	New Jerusalem built in America for the remnant of Joseph
History 1:27	Where carcass is (Christ), there the eagles gather
JD 2:57	Law of consecration fulfilled after Zion is redeemed
JD 3:18	Zion redeemed, New Jerusalem and temple built, before Christ comes
JD 15:364	Lord leads saints back to Jackson County like children of Israel
JD 15:338	Lord to come to temple in Zion (America) and will dwell in Zion for a long time prior to going to Jerusalem
JD 17:330	When temple built, all who enter will see the Lord
JD 21:136	Zion purchased quietly, because saints are rich
JD 24:29	Light of city is so bright, no sun needed, fill others with terror
Heber C. Kimball	After gospel given to Jews, return to Jackson County
Mil Mess 304	There are two "New Jerusalems," the city built by the saints and the city of Enoch that comes down from heaven
Mil Mess 305–3306	New Jerusalem starts prior to the coming of Christ, then

Christ comes, then after earth is cleansed and becomes terrestrial, Enoch comes

Nations Gather to War Against Israel

Joel 3:1, 2, 9	When Judah returns, all nations gather, prepare for war
Ezekiel 38:15	Army will come from the north
Ezekiel 38:16	Army covers the land like a cloud
Zechariah 12:2–3	Jerusalem a burdensome stone, all gather against
Revelation 9:16	Size of army 200 million
Joseph Smith	When the great bear (Russia) lays her paw on the lion (Britain), the winding up scene is not far distant.
Mil Mess 448	No nation will be neutral

Adam-Ondi-Ahman

Article of Faith 10	Christ will reign personally upon the earth
D&C 107:53–57	Previous meeting at Adam-Ondi-Ahman
D&C 116	Spring Hill, Missouri, place where Adam will visit his people
Daniel 7:9–14	Ancient of days gives dominion to Son of man
Daniel 7:21–22	Anti-Christ prevails until Ancient of days comes
Joel 2:15–18	Solemn assembly and fast is held in Zion prior to the Lord and His army coming to save Jews
Malachi 3:1	The Lord shall suddenly come to His temple
Revelation 7:9	Council so large no one can count
Doc of Sal 3:14	Prophets back to Adam give Christ keys to the kingdom
TPJS 157	Adam give Christ dominion over the earth
Mil Mess 578	Secret meeting first, then all members, and sacrament meeting
Mil Mess 586	All members must sustain Christ as head of the church

144,000

D&C 77:11	Will be high priests ordained to bring people to the Church of the Firstborn
D&C 133:18	Lord stands on Mount Zion with 144,000
Revelation 7:1–4	Hurt not the earth until 144,000 called and sealed
Revelation 7:16	Translated so that they cannot be hurt
Revelation 7:34	Destroying angels sent after 144,000 sealed
Revelation 14:1	144,000 to go with Christ to Mount Zion
History 6:365	144,000 saviors on Mount Zion
JD 15:365–366	144,000 protected from destruction while preaching

Testimony of Disasters

D&C 77:12	Sounding of trumpets finish His work, prepare for His coming
D&C 88:89–90	After testimony of elders comes testimony of earthquakes, tempests, tidal waves, etc.; all earth in commotion
D&C 112:25–26	To begin within the church and from within outward
Doc of Sal 3:7	Disasters follow nations rejecting the gospel
Doc of Sal 3:34	Saints to escape plagues by obedience
1 Nephi 22:16, 19	God will not suffer the wicked to destroy the righteous, the righteous need not fear, they shall not perish
Moses 7:61	But my people will I preserve
Matthew JST 33	After abomination of desolation (Anti-Christ takes over the temple), sun and moon dark, stars fall, powers of heaven shaken
Revelation 7:34	Destroying angels sent out after 144,000 sealed
Revelation 16:2–17	Seven plagues, seven angels, seven trumpets
Mil Mess 634	Coming of Christ and resurrection prior to plagues and judgment

First Woe: A star falls from heaven

The effects of the tail of the comet

Revelation 8:7	Hail, fire and blood cast upon the earth; 1/3 trees and all grass die
Revelation 16:2	Evil sore upon men which had mark of the beast, island moved, every mountain brought down
D&C 29:16	Great hailstorm destroys crops of the earth
D&C 109:30	Evil works swept away by the hail and judgment

The effects of the head of the comet

Revelation 8:8–9	Mountain burning with fire (volcano) cast into the sea: 1/3 of sea polluted, 1/3 of sea life dies, 1/3 of ships destroyed (volcanoes)
Revelation 9:1–11	Plague of locusts hurt only those with mark of beast, torment so great men seek death
Revelation 16:3–4	Upon the sea and rivers: turn to blood, all waters polluted, all life dies
Revelation 16:10	Plague upon Satan's kingdom, men blaspheme God because of pain, do not repent
D&C 61:4–5	No flesh safe on the water

The comet hits the earth

Revelation 8:10–11	Star falls from heaven, 1/3 of rivers/water polluted, many die from drinking the water

Earth is moved from its orbit

D&C 88:87	Earth to reel to and fro, sun darkened, moon to blood, stars fall
Isaiah 13:10	Sun, moon, stars lose their light
Isaiah 13:13	Heavens shake, earth moved out of her place
Isaiah 24:20	Earth to fall, reel to and fro
Joel 2:10	Earth trembles; sun, moon, stars darkened
Revelation 8:12	One-third of sun, moon, stars darkened
Revelation 16:8	Men scorched with heat (earth falls towards sun)
JD 1:130	Earth to fall and begin journey back to Kolob

Note: as earth recedes from sun, turns red and darkness

Second Woe: The Battle of Armageddon

Revelation 6:12	Great earthquake, sun black, moon red, stars fall
Revelation 9:12	One woe is past, two woes to come
Revelation 9:14–16	Four evil men gather army of 200 million, slay 1/3 of all men living, men do not repent
Revelation 9:17–18	Fire, smoke, brimstone—by these three 1/3 of men killed (atomic warfare)
Revelation 11:2	Siege to last 3 1/2 years
Revelation 16:12	Three men work miracles, gather nations to battle
Revelation 19:19	Anti-Christ and army fight Christ
Ezekiel 38:2–7	Nations to come against Israel from the north: Meshech, Tubal, Persia, Ethiopia, Gomer, Togarmah, etc.
Ezekiel 38:15–16	Army will come from the north, covers land like a cloud
Ezekiel 38:21	Every man's sword shall be against his brother
Zechariah 12:2	Army lays siege against Jerusalem
Zechariah 12:3	All people gather to fight against Jerusalem
Zechariah 13:7–9	Two-thirds of Jews dead, rest to be purified by Christ
Zechariah 14:2–3	Lord to fight against all nations gathered to Jerusalem, Jerusalem taken and plundered, women savaged, half the city led captive
Zechariah 14:4–9	Mount of Olives cleaves in twain, no night during battle, water to come from Jerusalem, Lord becomes King of whole earth
Deuteronomy 28:53	During siege women eat their children, fathers eat sons
Matthew JST 21	Again shall the abominations of desolation be fulfilled
Joel 2:1–11	Lord's army destroys and burns everything—total destruction
Joel 2:30–31	Wonders in heaven and earth: blood, fire, pillars of smoke, sun darkened, moon to blood (atomic warfare)
McConkie	Use of nuclear weapons inevitable

Joseph Fielding Smith	Bombs will not reach Zion
Doc of Sal 3:46	Will end all nations, will end at siege of Jerusalem
D&C 1:35	Peace taken from the earth, devil has power over his dominion

Two Prophets

Zechariah 4:14	Two anointed ones
Zechariah 12:9	Grace of God on Jerusalem, God will destroy all nations
Revelation 11:3	Power given to two witnesses for 260 days
Revelation 11:6	Have power to perform great miracles
Revelation 11:7–8	Beast shall kill them, bodies lay in the street three days
Revelation 11:9–10	All people shall see their dead bodies and celebrate
Revelation 11:12–12	At Christ's coming they are resurrected in view of all
Revelation 11:13	Great earthquake destroys city and people
Revelation 13:5	Anti-Christ given power 42 months or 3 1/2 years
2 Nephi 8:18–19	Two sons sent, not of the Jews
D&C 45:26	Wars, whole earth in commotion
D&C 77:15	Two prophets raised up to prophesy to the Jews
Mil Mess 390	Two witnesses after temple built, they will be two apostles
Daniel 8:11–14	Anti-Christ takes over temple and rules earth for 6 1/2 years
Daniel 8:25	Anti-Christ challenges God for possession of the earth, but will lose
Daniel 12:11–12	From time Anti-Christ takes possession of the temple to the coming of Christ is 3 1/2 years; 45 days later, war is over

Note: Daniel 9:27 and Revelation 12:6, 14 seem to say there will be a total of 7 years of tribulation: 3 1/2 years beginning of sorrows (Matthew 24:8), 3 1/2 years end of sorrows, great tribulation (Matthew 24:21)

Note: Scriptures seem to indicate that the rapture will occur prior to the worst of the tribulations:

- ◆ 1 Thess. 5:4   not in darkness that this day should overtake us
- ◆ 1 Thess. 5:9   not appointed to wrath
- ◆ Romans 5:9   saved from wrath
- ◆ Revelation 12:6, 14   woman (church) flees 1260 days or 3 1/2 years

Silence in Heaven

Revelation 8:1	After opening of seventh seal, there was silence in heaven for a half hour
D&C 1:35	House when peace taken from the earth and devil has power
D&C 38:12	Silence caused by wickedness as, darkness prevails
D&C 88:95	Silence in heaven half hour after trump and prior to Christ's coming

Third Woe: Jesus Christ
The Sign of Christ

D&C 29:11	Christ revealed with all the hosts of heaven to dwell 1,000 years
D&C 45:44	Comes in clouds of heaven with all the Holy angels
D&C 88:93	Immediately a great sign appears, all people see it
Matthew JST 24:36	After the tribulation, after sun and moon dark, shall appear the sign of the Son of man in heaven, and then all will see Christ coming
Revelation 1:7	He cometh in the clouds, every eye shall see, men will wail
TPJS 287	One grand sign, men will say it is a comet
Doc of Sal 3:3	Christ shall come at the appointed time
Mil Mess 230	There will be man appearances which are the second coming

Trump Sounds

D&C 29:13	Trump, earthquake, dead arise
D&C 77:6, 12	Christ comes at seventh trump, beginning of seventh trump is 1,000 year period
D&C 88:92	Angels fly through heaven, sounding trump; bridegroom cometh
D&C 88:98	Resurrection by sound of the trump
D&C 109:75	Trump sounds for the dead
Matthew JST 24:37	Christ sends His angels before Him with great sound of a trump, to gather His elect
Mil Mess 389	Last battle starts after seventh trumpet

Face of God Unveiled

D&C 38:8	Veil of darkness shall be rent
D&C 88:95	Heaven unfolded as a scroll, face of God unveiled
D&C 101:23	Veil taken off, all flesh see Christ together
Revelation 6:14–16	Heaven depart as a scroll, rocks fall on us
JD 18:170	Even dead shall see His coming

Saints Caught Up

D&C 29:11–12	Christ revealed, 12 apostles at right hand, will judge house of Israel
D&C 29:13	Trump, earthquake, first resurrection
D&C 45:45	Saints meet Christ in the air
D&C 76:102	Those caught up are Church of Firstborn
D&C 88:96	Graves opened, saints caught up in midst of pillar of heaven
D&C 88:98	Saints shall descend with Christ
D&C 109:74	Mountains flow down at thy presence, valleys exalted
D&C 133:18	Lamb shall stand on Mount Zion with 144,000

D&C 133:49	So great Christ's glory, sun hide, moon dark, stars fall
Moses 7:63	City of Enoch hears Christ's voice and returns
Matthew 24:44–45	One left in field, one taken
1 Thess. 4:16–17	Lord descends with a shot, dead arise first, then saints caught up
Jude 14	Lord comes with 10,000 saints
Revelation 3:12	Name of God's city is New Jerusalem, cometh down from heaven
Revelation 16:17	Thunder, lightning, great earthquake—greatest ever—cities fall, every
Moses 7:63	Saints taken up, meet City of Enoch in the air
JD 8:51	City of Enoch comes with Abraham
JD 8:52	After saints caught up, tables spread and sacrament given
JD 10:147–148	When Enoch descends, Zion ascends to meet them
Doc of Sal 2:296	Church of Firstborn caught up, then first resurrection
Mil Mess 304	City of Enoch comes back after earth is made terrestrial
Mil Mess 393	One great earthquake, all land leveled earth united
Mil Mess 627	They are resurrected saints from ages past
Mil Mess 634	First resurrection prior to plagues and judgment

Arm of the Lord falls upon the Nations (Christ and army go to Jerusalem)

D&C 29:9	All proud and wicked as stubble, Lord will burn them up
D&C 29:21	Great and abominable church cast down by devouring fire
D&C 45:47	After resurrection, arm of Lord falls upon the nations
D&C 45:48	Great earthquake, Mount of Olives cleaves in twain, earth reels
D&C 45:50	Those in iniquity hews down and cast into the fire
D&C 87:6	All nations come to an end
D&C 133:20	After Mount Zion, Lord shall stand on Olivet
D&C 133:41	Presence of Lord a fire that burneth, that causes water to boil
D&C 133:48	Christ red in apparel
D&C 133:62	Wicked to burn as stubble
Isaiah 2:19	They shall go into holes of rocks and caves for fear of the Lord
Isaiah 13:14–15	Description of last battle, stars, moon, sun darkened
Isaiah 34:2–5	Lord destroys armies of all nations, heaven roll together as a scroll
Isaiah 63:1–2	Who comes with dyed garments, red with blood
Isaiah 63:4	Day of vengeance, Lord comes in anger
Isaiah 66:15–16	Lord comes with fire, by fire and sword the Lord will slay wicked
Isaiah 66:19	Those that escape declare Lord's glory to gentile nations
Psalms 50:3–5	God comes and fire devours before Him

2 Thess 1:7	Lord and angels in flaming fire take vengeance
Matthew JST 55	The end of the wicked as Moses: they shall be cut off from among the people; but the end of the earth I not yet
Revelation 14:1	144,000 to go with Christ to Mount of Olives
Revelation 16:19	Greatest earthquake ever, city divided into three parts
Revelation 16:21	Hail falls upon men (weight 57 lbs) men blasphemed God
Revelation 17:16–17	Nations turn against Anti-Christ and each other
Revelation 19:11–21	Christ comes on a white horse, with red garments, and destroys the beast and his army
Joel 2:1–11	Description of Lord's army
Joel 3:18	A fountain shall come forth of the house of the Lord
Ezekiel 38:19–20	All earth, seven seas, every creature to shake at His presence, mountains thrown down
Ezekiel 38:21	Every man's sword shall be against his brother
Ezekiel 38:22	Hailstones rain upon army, fire and brimstone
Ezekiel 39:6	Fire destroys rest of wicked
Ezekiel 47:1, 8	Waters issue from under temple, heal Dead Sea
Zechariah 14:3	Lord comes to fight
Zechariah 14:4	Large valley created, running east and west
Zechariah 14:5	Lord comes with all the saints
Zechariah 14:6–7	Will not get dark until armies are destroyed
Zechariah 14:8	Spring of water comes out of temple, heals Dead Sea
Zechariah 14:18	They shall hold every one on the hand of his neighbor
Mil Mess 448	Fountain of water from under temple, for baptism of Jews
Mil Mess 525	Burning at Christ's coming will be literal fire that consumes, righteous will be like Shadrach, Meshach and Obednago in the furnace and escape
Doc of Sal 3:9	Wicked burned as stubble
Doc of Sal 3:44	Destruction of wicked an act of mercy
History 2:37	Fire equals glory
Bks of Eden 152:14–17	Inexhaustible supply of water from within the temple, water from the base of the altar to wash away the sacrifices

Jews Converted

D&C 45:51–53	What are these wounds? Jews look on Christ and are converted
D&C 133:35	Tribe of Judah to be sanctified
Zechariah 12:10	They shall look upon me whom they have pierced
Zechariah 13:6	What are these wounds?
Zechariah 13:9	One-third of Jews left alive
Doc of Sal 3:8	Christ to convert Jews

Final Plague

D&C 29:18–19	Plague of flies and maggots (because of dead bodies from war)
Ezekiel 39:2	Army struck with six plagues
Zechariah 14:12	Plague sent, consumes flesh of remaining army

Supper of the Great God

D&C 29:20	Beasts and fowls devour army
Ezekiel 39:4, 17–20	Dead devoured by beasts
Revelation 19:17–18	Birds and beasts eat dead

Christ appears to all people

D&C 45:49	Lord will utter His voice, ends of earth to hear, nations mourn
D&C 133:20	Christ shows Himself to oceans, islands, Zion
D&C 133:21	Lord's voice heard among all people
D&C 133:22–23	Lord's voice breaks down mountains, oceans driven back, all lands become one
Isaiah 65:17–25	Earth changed to a terrestrial state
Matthew 24:26	Christ's coming like light of morning spread from east to west
Revelation 16:20	Earth becomes one land mass, mountains broken down

Millennium

Article of Faith 10	Earth renewed to paradisiacal glory
D&C 45:58	Earth an inheritance, children grow up without sin to salvation
D&C 101:26	Enmity of man, beast, all things, shall cease
D&C 101:27	Whatsoever any man ask will give given
D&C 101:28	Satan to have no power to tempt any man
D&C 101:29	No sorrow, no death
D&C 101:30	Infant not die until old as tree, changed in twinkling of an eye
D&C 101:32	All things will be revealed
D&C 133:25	Lord in midst of His people, reign over all flesh
D&C 133:29	Living water to come forth out of barren deserts
D&C 133:45	Eye not seen, nor men heard, things prepared for the righteous
Moses 7:64–65	Earth to rest, Christ to dwell 1,000 years
2 Nephi 27:7–11	Sealed plates read by power of Christ
2 Nephi 30:10–15	Wolf to lay with lamb, child with asp, etc.
2 Nephi 30:16–18	The acts of nations made known, nothing secret, all things revealed

Isaiah 4:1	Polygamy: seven women take hold of one man (loss of men during war)
Isaiah 11:6–9	Wolf dwell with lamb, animals eat straw, etc.
Isaiah 65:17	Child not die, live to 100, build homes, plant vineyards, etc.
Joel 3:20	Dead will be buried in valley by east sea
Ezekiel 39:9–10	City dwellers burn weapons for fuel for seven years
Ezekiel 39:11–14	Men set apart to bury dead seven months, buried in large valley, stench
Micah 4:3	Shall beat swords into plowshares, etc., not fight or learn war
Zephaniah 3:9	People to have one pure language, to call upon and serve God
Zechariah 14:16–17	Nations go up every year to worship Christ or no rain upon them
Zechariah 14:21	No more Canaanite in House of the Lord
Revelation 11:15	The Kingdoms of this world become Christ's, there is time no longer
Revelation 18:11	No buying or selling of precious things, only necessities
JD 2:316	Zion covers whole earth, but permits different beliefs
Mil Mess 113	Add to Bible, plates of brass, sealed plates of Nephi, etc. come forth
Mil Mess 655	Polygamy reinstated
Mil Mess 658	All life to be vegetarians, no death, no blood
Mil Mess 674	All faithful to receive calling and election, second comforter
Doc of Sal 3:11	Christ to purify and change earth back to Garden of Eden
Doc of Sal 3:56	Earth and everything in it is changed
Doc of Sal 3:59	Christ and resurrected will not stay on earth
Doc of Sal 3:63	Celestial and terrestrial living, there will be wicked men on earth who believe different, but must boy to Christ and His laws

Righteous led to Zion and Jerusalem

D&C 133:26–27	Prophets hear Christ, use Priesthood to come to Zion
D&C 133:30	Nations to bring riches to Ephraim in Zion
D&C 133:32–34	Those who come, crowned by Ephraim, greater blessings on Ephraim
JD 16:325–326	Ten tribes gather after Christ comes
JD 18:25	John prepares ten tribes for their return
Mil Mess 216	Gathering of ten tribes after Christ comes

Second Trump

| D&C 45:54 | Heathen nations redeemed, part of first resurrection |
| D&C 88:99 | Second trump begins first resurrection, spirit prison |

Third Trump

D&C 76:81–81	Telestial thrust into hell until last resurrection
D&C 88:110	Wicked judged, remain in hell until after millennium
D&C 133:64–73	Wicked cast into outer darkness, weeping, gnashing of teeth
Doc of Sal 3:59, 62	Wicked remain in spirit prison, those living telestial laws

Fourth Trump

D&C 29:10	Dwell in righteousness 1,000 years
D&C 43:31	Satan bound, then loosed, then the end of the earth
D&C 45:55	Satan bound, no place in the hearts of men
D&C 88:102	Satan bound, time no longer, Sons of Perdition judged
D&C 101:28	Satan has no power to tempt any man
1 Nephi 22:15, 26	Satan has no power because of the righteousness of the people
Revelation 20:2	Satan bound 1,000 years

Fifth Trump

D&C 88:103	Commits gospel to all nations and people
D&C 88:104	Everyone accepts and kneels before Christ
Mosiah 16:1	Ever nation to accept Christ
Mosiah 27:31	Every knee bow, every tongue confess Christ

Sixth Trump

D&C 88:105	Christ and kingdom of God rules the earth
Matthew JST 31	Gospel preached to all the world, then the end of the world comes
Doc of Sal 3:64	Gospel taught until all inhabitants embrace it

Seventh Trump

D&C 88:106	It is finished
D&C 88:107	Saints receive their inheritance, made equal with Christ
D&C 88:108–110	Trumps repeat, reveal the acts of men, all things revealed

Final Trump (end of the millennium)

D&C 29:22	End of 1,000 years, men deny God, earth spared a little season
D&C 29:26	Michael to sound trump, rest of the dead awake
D&C 43:31	Satan loosed a little season, then cometh end of the earth
D&C 88:111	Satan loosed, gathers army
D&C 88:112	Michael gathers together the host of heaven

D&C 88:113	Satan gathers army, comes to battle
Revelation 20:3, 8	Satan loosed to deceive nations, gather them to battle
Mil Mess 536, 695	Little season equals 1,000 years

Battle of the Great God

D&C 29:27	Righteous on right hand, wicked on left, wicked sent to everlasting fire
D&C 88:114	Devil and followers cast out by Michael
Revelation 20:8	Devil brings innumerable host to battle
Revelation 20:9	Armies surround City of Zion

Earth is baptized in fire; becomes Celestial

D&C 29:23	End shall come, heaven and earth consumed and pass away, new heaven and earth, all things made new: men, beast, fish, fowl
D&C 77:1–4	Sea of glass is the celestial earth
D&C 101:24–25	All corruption consumed, elements melt, all things new
1 Nephi 22:17	Earth destroyed as by fire
2 Nephi 26:3	Elements melt, earth wrap together as a scroll, heavens and earth pass away
Matthew JST 4	Destruction of the wicked is the end of the world
Jude 1:6	Angels which kept not first estate reserved in everlasting darkness
Jude 1:13	Wandering stars, for who is reserved blackness of darkness forever
2 Peter 3:7, 13	Heaven and earth reserved unto fire, new heaven and earth for the righteous
2 Peter 3:10	Elements melt, earth burned up
2 Thess. 1:7	Lord's angels in fire take vengeance
Revelation 4:6	Earth to become sea of glass
Revelation 20:9	Fire comes down from heaven, devours Satan and his armies
Revelation 21:1	A new heaven and earth, dies and is resurrected, no more sea
Ezekiel 39:6	Fire destroys wicked
Psalms 50:3–5	Fire shall devour before Him

Chronology of the Second Coming and Celestialization of the Earth[*]

GLOBAL	NEW WORLD	OLD WORLD
	1820–1830: Times of the Gentiles begins (Church established)	
		1948: Times of the Jews begins (Nation of Israel established)
1978: Times of the Heathen Nations begins (Priesthood given to all worthy males)		
		Solomon's Temple rebuilt in Jerusalem
		Second Woe (all wars associated with the Anti-Christ up to and including the Battle of Armageddon) Rise of the Anti-Christ and his 3 "prophets." There are wars to consolidate this power as he builds a coalition with ten other nations
Rejection and recalling of missionaries		
	United States government falls	

[*] Created by Christopher Hopkins

The Second Coming of Jesus Christ

GLOBAL	NEW WORLD	OLD WORLD
	The Saints gather to Zion and live under the law of consecration by reestablishing the United Order	
	Temple built in New Jerusalem	
Millennium begins	General Conference held in Adam-ondi-Ahman to release the Prophet and sustain Christ as the leader of the church ♦ Saints expand New Jerusalem to provide for the resurrection of the Church of the Firstborn ♦ 144,000 High Priests are called to prepare saints to receive their calling and election ♦ An army of righteous are gathered and trained to destroy the Anti-Christ and his host	Anti-Christ continues to gain power; all nations eventually side *against* Israel except for the United States
Testimony of Disasters First Woe (a comet hits the earth) ♦ 1st trump: Hail mixed with fire and blood (the comet's tail brushing the earth's surface) ♦ 2nd trump: Burning mountain hits ocean (the comet collides with the earth with such force that it is knocked out of orbit and begins a journey to Kolob) ♦ 3rd trump: $1/3$ of the earth's water becomes undrinkable		

GLOBAL	NEW WORLD	OLD WORLD

♦ 4th trump: ⅓ of the earth is darkened from all sun, moon and stars
  ♦ 1st vial (plague): those who follow Satan are afflicted by sores which leave the mark of the beast
  ♦ 2nd vial: seas turn to blood thus killing all sea life
  ♦ 3rd vial: rivers and waters turned to blood
  ♦ 4th vial: earth scorched with heat as it passes the sun on its way to Kolob
♦ 5th trump: plague of insects afflict the wicked		

		6th trump: Anti-Christ and his forces of 200,000,000 march against Jerusalem
	Christ sends two prophets to Jerusalem	The "Siege of Jerusalem" which lasts 3½ years.
		The hand of the Lord is withdrawn from Jerusalem ♦ The two prophets are killed and left in the street for 3 days ♦ The Anti-Christ overruns the city ♦ The Anti-Christ desecrates temple by using it as his personal throne

135

GLOBAL	NEW WORLD	OLD WORLD
Third Woe (Jesus Christ)		
"Great Sign in Heaven" 1st trump: *The Morning of the First Resurrection* Christ in His glory, along with Michael, all of the Saints who were resurrected with Christ, the City of Enoch (including the land mass), and the hosts of angels assigned to earth will descend from the sky. Those who will be of the "Church of the Firstborn" (those who will gain exaltation) that are not descending with Him will rise to meet Him either resurrected from their graves or quickened from life. Only the righteous will understand the significance of this comet-like ball of light descending from the heavens. Mountains move and the earth shakes with the greatest earthquake the world has ever known; the continents begin to move together again. They settle in the land of New Jerusalem while the land mass of the City of Enoch resumes its proper place in the Gulf of Mexico.		The prophets left dead in the streets of Jerusalem are resurrected and taken up to meet the descending Savior
Half hour of silence		
	Those who will form the *Army of the World* are set apart and prepared to battle the Anti-Christ and his army	
	The resurrected and transfigured beings who comprise the *Army of the Lord* march on Jerusalem destroying everyone and everything in its path, cleansing and burning the earth	

GLOBAL	NEW WORLD	OLD WORLD
		The war ensues between the *Army of the Lord* and the Anti-Christ and his army, culminating in the Battle of Armageddon. The resulting carnage is so great that 200 square miles of land are covered with blood so deep as to come up to a horse's bridle.
		After vanquishing the Anti-Christ of the army, Christ enters Jerusalem as an earthquake causes the Mount of Olives to divide, thus allowing Christ and His army to approach the temple from the east. This earthquake frees an underground water source to cleanse the temple, baptize the Jews and heal the Dead Sea.
		In coming upon the city as a military savior, the Jews, only about 1/3 who live in Jerusalem have survived the war, line the streets to honor their liberator only to realize that He is Jesus Christ, who they crucified many years before. They accept him as their Savior and are baptized.
One final plague is wrought upon the remnants of the Anti-Christ's fleeing army and the other wicked who remain		
"The Supper of the Great God" Animals and birds feast upon the dead strewn throughout the world		

GLOBAL	NEW WORLD	OLD WORLD
The righteous, at the direction of the Lord and His leaders, begin the process of cleansing the earth of war's destruction to bring it to a terrestrial state, as was the Garden of Eden.		
Christ and His annointed call upon the world's inhabitants to obey the laws of the new theocratic government established by God with Christ as His King		
The earth is cleansed and achieves a terrestrial state		
Christ and those who are prepared for a higher existence leave this earth		
2nd trump: Indicates the end of the morning of the 1st resurrection (or the end of the resurrection of the "Church of the Firstborn") and the beginning of the first part of the general resurrection. These are they of the heathen nations and those of a terrestrial nature.		
3rd trump: Judgment is made upon the wicked; the end of the first resurrection.		
4th trump: Those that are living are righteous and have rejected Satan; Satan is bound.		
5th trump: The kingdom of God controls the earth as all living have personally accepted Christ and covenants to obey His laws		

GLOBAL	NEW WORLD	OLD WORLD
6th trump: All living have converted to the Gospel of Jesus Christ. The Great and Abominable Church (false doctrine) has been defeated		
7th trump: Christ has triumphed because all of the work of the righteous has been completed: all have been converted, all of the temple work has been done, and all of the righteous (both celestial and terrestrial) have been resurrected		
Millennium ends Christ ends His personal reign upon the earth		
The resurrection of the wicked, or those to be found in the Telestial Kingdom		
Satan loosed for 1000 years. Those that sin and fall during this period become Sons of Perdition because they have a perfect knowledge of the Savior and His gospel. As there are none of our Heavenly Father's spirit children left, wombs are closed and no children are born.		

The Second Coming of Jesus Christ

GLOBAL	NEW WORLD	OLD WORLD
"The Battle of the Great God" A second "Battle of Armageddon" where the wicked are destroyed by a celestial fire. The bodies of the wicked, the Sons of Perdition, are physically burned away in a "Second Death." They become spirits once again, as is their master, Satan. The wicked spirits, including Satan, are sealed into a bottomless pit (a black hole) and revert back to simple intelligences. This fire also changes the earth from a terrestrial to a celestial state of existence. The earth, a living being, gains its own celestial glory as it finally arrives at Kolob and becomes a Urim and Thummim.		

Index